Hacking with Kali Linux

A Beginner's Guide to Learning All the Basics
of Kali Linux and Cyber Security: Includes
Network Defense Strategies, Penetration
Testing, and Hacking Tools for Computer

Table of Contents

Introduction... 1

Chapter : 1 Brief Overview of Hacking 2

Chapter : 2 Kali Linux Installation 17

Chapter : 3 Hardware Hacking Using Linux........................... 48

Chapter : 4 Network Security 72

Chapter : 5 Social Engineering.. 85

Chapter : 6 Network Scanning and Management................. 93

Chapter : 7 Cryptography 109

Chapter : 8 Cyber Security 117

Chapter : 9 Virtual Private Network and Firewall 137

Chapter : 10 Password Cracking.. 149

Conclusion 158

Introduction

This book is not intended for the experienced hacker or the experienced Linux admin. Instead, it is intended for those who want to get started along the exciting path of hacking, cybersecurity, and pen testing. It is also intended not as a complete treatise on Linux or hacking, but rather a starting point into these worlds. It begins with the essentials of Linux and extends into some basic scripting in both bash and Python. Wherever appropriate, I have tried to use examples from the world of hacking to teach Linux principles.

In this introduction, we'll look at the growth of ethical hacking for information security, and I'll take you through the process of installing a virtual machine, so you can install Kali Linux on your system without disturbing the operating system you are already running.

Chapter : 1
Brief Overview of Hacking

Hacking Definition

This is a process of identification of flaws that are present in a given network or computer systems that can be used to exploit its weaknesses to gain access.

An excellent hacking example is employing the use of a password cracking algorithm to secure entry into a system. In this age, computers are indispensable when it comes to running successful businesses. Additionally, computers need to be networked to be able to facilitate the exchange of communication with other external businesses. This means that isolated computer systems, on their own, are not enough. By networking them, it means that we are exposing them to the outside world, and thus making it possible for them to get hacked. Hacking essentially implies the use of computers to carry out malicious acts, for instance, stealing personal or corporate data, privacy invasion, fraud, and so on. Cybercrimes are known to cost organizations all around the world millions of dollars each year.

It is, therefore, prudent that businesses protect themselves against such attacks. Most of the hacking worldwide are carried out with criminal intent. This can range from committing some form of fraud to ruining the reputation of the targeted organization. Hackers can steal crucial data, embezzle funds, and even spread misleading or malicious information that can be detrimental socially. Hacking is a crime and is, in most jurisdictions, punishable by law. In spite of this, there is a form of hacking that is considered beneficial. This is done by professionals, government law agencies, and other accredited institutions. Primarily, they intend to counter the malevolent intent of malicious hackers. This way, it is possible to safeguard systems against harm. The protection and safety of the general society and its citizens can be achieved by this type of professional hacking, otherwise known as ethical hacking.

Common Hacker Attacks

The following are the most common types of hacker attacks against computers and networks.

1. Denial of Service (DoS) Attack

A websites' server can get overloaded when it is flooded by traffic more than it can handle. Picture this, a road designed to handle traffic from a small town can quickly get gridlocked when there is an influx of external traffic. The users will experience massive delays, and the inconvenience will be great. This is how a denial of service attack affect websites. The additional traffic on the site will make it impossible to provide service to visitors who are trying to access it.

A practical example is a newspaper's website carrying breaking news. Many people will try to access it to find out more consequently overloading the site. In a DoS attack, however, the overloaded traffic is ordinarily malicious. The intention is to shut down the website from its legitimate users. A Distributed Denial-of-Service Attack (DDoS) is an attack carried out by many computers at the same time. It is challenging to cope with this type of attack since the IP addresses will appear to be originating from many different locations around the world simultaneously. This means that it is difficult to determine the source of attack by network administrators.

2. Cross-Site Scripting (XSS)

An attacker can go after a vulnerable website in an SQL injection attack. Stored data can be targeted. For instance, sensitive financial data, user credentials, among others. A cross-site scripting attack is preferable to an attacker who would instead directly target a website's users. Just like an SQL injection attack, a cross-site scripting attack involves injecting malicious code into a site. The only difference is that the website itself is not being attacked. What happens is that a malicious attacker will carry out an injection on the user's browser upon visiting the infected site. A common way to do this is by injecting the code which is malicious into a comment or a script that could automatically run. For instance, in JavaScript, a link can be embedded in a comment on a blog. This type of attack can, in essence, damage a website's reputation by risking users' information without necessarily doing anything malicious. In some cases, sensitive information users transmit on the site can be hijacked through cross-site scripting before even the owners of the website realize that there is a problem.

3. SQL Injection Attack

SQL is a programming language we use to communicate with databases. Most servers doing storage of critical data for websites and services usually utilize SQL for the management of data that is stored on their databases. This type of assault targets precisely this kind of server. It employs the use of malicious code to prompt the server to disclose the information it would not normally do. The problem can be amplified if the server is used for storing private customer details, for example, usernames, numbers of credit cards, and so on. This information can be used to identify a person. The attack carries out its intended goal through the exploitation of any one of the known SQL vulnerabilities that are known to permit running malicious codes on the SQL server. For instance, an injection - attack - vulnerable SQL server may motivate an attacker to type in a code in the website's search box which will make the SQL server of the site dump the usernames and passwords that have been stored for the site.

4. Phishing

A good number of phishing scams come in the form of text message and email campaigns that are meant to create a feeling of curiosity, compelling urgency, or even instill fear in potential casualties. The victims are then prodded into disclosing information that is deemed sensitive, following the links to malicious websites by clicking on them, or by downloading and opening unknown attachments containing malware. For instance, users of a particular online service can receive an email that alerts them of a policy violation that requires an action to be done immediately on their part. An example of such a move is a password change. Upon clicking the link, the user will be redirected to an illegitimate website that is almost identical in every aspect as the legitimate one, prompting an unsuspecting user to input his or her credentials to the site. That information is sent to the attacker once the form is submitted.

5. Malware

Attackers usually prefer to deploy malware in a users' computer so that they are in a position to gain a foothold there. It is one of the most effective ways of gaining access. First, let us define what malware is. It can be said to represent various configurations of software that are harmful, for instance: ransomware and viruses. A malware present in your computer is capable of wreaking all sorts of havoc. This includes but is not limited to the following: monitoring and recording actions and keystrokes you perform on your computer, assuming control of your machine, and even sending your confidential data to the attacker's base directly from your computer. There are many ways through whichan attacker can deliver malware into your computer. However, for this to work, it will require that the user, on their own volition, take action to install the malware such as opening an attachment looking harmless or clicking a link to download a particular file all of which contain hidden malware in them.

6. Session Hijacking and Man-in-the-Middle Attacks

The computer you are using typically make numerous back-and-forth transactions with the servers around the world to inform them of your identity and the specific websites or services that you are requesting whenever you are on the internet. If all goes well, you will get all the information that you had requested from the web servers. This is the norm both when you are logging into a particular website with your credentials, that is, the username and password or just simply browsing. A unique session ID is given to the session between the remote web server and your computer. That ID needs to stay private. When an attacker comes into the picture, they can use the obtained session ID's to hijack the session.

That is made possible through capturing the session ID and feigning resemblance to the computer making a request. The attacker can log in the same way as an unsuspecting user would do and as such, obtain access to crucial information on the webserver. We have several ways an attacker can employ to be able to steal the session ID. One of them is a cross-site scripting attack that we have discussed before. Alternatively, the attacker may decide to do session hijacking by placing themselves in between the remote server and the requesting computer. Here, they will be pretending to be the other party involved in the session. This way, they will be able to intercept information being transmitted from both directions. This is what we refer to as a man-in-the-middle attack.

7. Password attack

The commonly used method of authentication of users to any information system is the use of passwords. This means that stealing passwords is an effective approach that can be used in the attack. To do this, all it takes is to look around a targets' desk then carry out a sniffing operation on the connection. This will enable you to obtain unencrypted passwords. Here, one can use social engineering tactics to gain access to a database containing passwords or do outright guesswork to get the password. This can be carried out in either a random or systematic fashion. We have the following types of password attacks, brute-force attacks, and dictionary-based attacks. In the former type of attack, different passwords are tried randomly with the hope one of the combinations will work. An attacker can apply some logic to this procedure, such as trying passwords that relate to a users' name, hobbies, job title, and so on.

On the other hand, a dictionary-based attack utilizes common passwords found in a dictionary in their attempt to access a target's network or computer. A commonly used technique is whereby an encrypted file containing passwords is copied, and then similar encryption is applied to the password dictionary. The passwords are then compared. To safeguard oneself against a dictionary or a brute-force attack, all that is required is to put in place an account lockout policy. This will mean that a particular account will be locked after exceeding a specified number of attempted logins.

8. Eavesdropping attack

This attack is carried out by intercepting the traffic on the network. Through the use of eavesdropping, a malicious user will be able to get access to credit card numbers, passwords alongside other information that is deemed to be confidential in which the user may be exchanged over the network. We can either have a passive or an active eavesdropping attack. Let us briefly look at what they are.

Passive eavesdropping – In this mode of eavesdropping, a malicious user will attempt to obtain information by way of listening in on the messages being transmitted over the network.

Active eavesdropping — Information being transmitted is actively captured by way of an attacker disguising as if they were a friendly unit. This is carried out through querying the data transmitters. We call this scanning, tampering, or simply probing.

It is prudent to note that the detection of passive eavesdropping attacks is crucial. This is because it is a precursor to the active attacks. Data encryption is the best countermeasure for eavesdropping.

What are the types of hackers?

Let us differentiate the different types of hackers we are likely to encounter below. You will notice that each category of hackers possesses different objectives. We will also look at the various roles and goals each of the hackers has.

a) **Black hat hacker**

Commonly known as black hats, they usually have extensive knowledge regarding the various methods about bypassing security protocols and breaking into computer networks. Malware is generally written by black hats to help gain access to these systems. A black hats' main goal is usually to make a personal or financial gain. Some of them do carry out cyber espionage while some do it for fun. This category of hackers ranges from inexperienced amateurs whose idea of fun is spreading malware to those that are experienced whose objectives are to embezzle privileged data. Many a time, it is financial information they seek. They are also interested in harvesting login credentials and personal information.

Besides stealing data, they usually alter or sometimes destroy the data they have obtained if it does not serve their purpose.

b) Grey hat hacker

These can be said to be neither the bad or good guys! Grey hats are neither white nor black. This category of hackers has the characteristics of both black hats and white hats. Most of the time, grey hats will attempt to unearth, without the permission or knowledge of the owners, vulnerabilities that are present in a system. If they discover an issue, they will report the same to the owners. Most of the time, they will ask for some financial compensation so that they can fix the problem. In the 'unfortunate' event that the owner does not comply, they will go ahead and post their exploits on the internet for everyone to see. Grey hats' intentions are not necessarily malicious; all they want is to make some dollars out of their discoveries. After finding vulnerabilities, grey hats will not usually exploit the vulnerabilities that they have unearthed. What makes this grey hacking illegal is the fact that no prior permission was sought from the owners of a particular system the hackers targeted. For the readers seeking to become hackers, it is essential to note that not all hackers are created equal. We have white hat hackers who are always trying to uncover and fix vulnerabilities before black hats find them. This way, we have a lot fewer cyber crimes now.

c) White hat hacker

Unlike the two previous types of hackers, white hat hackers are those that put their skills to good use. Their intentions are benevolent. These are the good guys. This group of hackers is commonly referred to as ethical hackers. They may be an organizations' employees or work as contractors in information security companies. They usually try to discover vulnerabilities in a system through hacking. The methods used in the hacking process are similar to those that black hats use, but there is one differentiating aspect. White hats first seek the owners' consent. This makes the hacking legal. White hat hackers usually carry out penetration tests; they do assess vulnerabilities and conduct in-place testing of a company's security systems. We even have certifications, training, courses, and conferences that are hosted ethical hacking.

What is Ethical Hacking?

We define ethical hacking as an approved implementation whereby there is bypassing of a systems' security that helps in the identification of threats and potential data breaches in a network. In this scenario, an organization that owns a particular network or system grants permission to cybersecurity experts to carry out such activities to test the defenses a system has put in place. This, therefore, implies that, unlike malicious hacking, ethical hacking is a legal process that has been planned and approved. The main goal of an ethical hacker is to scrutinize a particular network or system for weak points. It is via these weak points that malicious hackers use in their exploitation or destruction.

While at it, they do gather and perform an analysis of the information. This will help them in the planning process of the organization's IT infrastructure. In doing so, the security footprint will be significantly improved in a manner that it can withstand or divert attacks. The demand for ethical hacking has witnessed a dramatic increase in recent times due to the growth of the information security sector. Ethical hacking is also known as white hat hacking. Ethical hacking is the practice of attempting to infiltrate and exploit a system to find out its weaknesses so that it cat be better secured. We can categorize it into two broad classes. These are penetration testing; this is mostly for a legitimate information security firm, and hacking by intelligence agencies or a nation's military. There is a rising demand for hacking in both areas.

Penetration Testing

As organizations become increasingly security-conscious, and the cost of security breaches rises exponentially, many large organizations are beginning to contract out security services. One of these key security services is penetration testing. A penetration test is essentially a legal, commissioned hack to demonstrate the vulnerability of a firm's network and systems.

Generally, organizations conduct a vulnerability assessment first to find potential vulnerabilities in their network, operating systems, and services. I emphasize potential, as this vulnerability scan includes a significant number of false positives (things identified as vulnerabilities that really are not). It is the role of the penetration tester to attempt to hack, or penetrate, these vulnerabilities. Only then can the organization know whether the vulnerability is real and decide to invest time and money to close the vulnerability.

Espionage and Military

Cyber espionage can be said to be the practice of accessing information and secrets without the knowledge and permission of the entities being targeted. They can be ordinary individuals, rivals, competitors, groups, governments, or even enemies. The objectives here are broad. They can be political, economic, personal, or even military-related. The techniques used are diverse. Hackers can use malicious software, cracking techniques, proxy servers among others to attain their stated objectives. Espionage can be carried out online by professionals from their computer desks, or it can be done by infiltration using trained moles and conventional spies. In some circumstances, it can be carried by amateurish hackers with malicious intent and software programmers. It is common knowledge that every nation on earth carries out some form of cyber espionage or even cyber warfare, albeit covertly. Gathering intelligence on military activities of other countries has been made more cost-effective by hacking. Thus, a hacker has their place cut out in the defense systems of any nation.

Chapter : 2
Kali Linux Installation

Overview of Kali

Kali is a distribution of the Linux family which is established upon the Debian architecture and was purposely designed and made for auditing of security and carrying out Penetration Testing at an advanced level. This distribution has hundreds of tools geared towards numerous security-related tasks, for instance, Forensics tasks, Security research, Testing by penetration of various security systems, and reverse engineering among many others. Kali has been developed and is managed by Offensive Security, an information security company specializing in training security solutions. Kali evolved from BackTrack. BackTrack was also the software of the Linux distribution family and was also utilized in penetration testing.

Reasons why Linux is preferred by hackers

As part of our introduction, we are going to discuss five reasons why the Linux operating systems are a preferred choice for hackers.

a) aIt is an open-source software

Unlike the Windows operating system software, Linux distribution is open-source. A Linux user has access to the operating systems' source code. This means that one can manipulate and change a Linux operating system to suit their needs at will. Supposing the user wants to make a particular system operate in ways besides those it was originally intended to, the ability to manipulate and change the source code is of paramount importance.

b) The operating system is transparent

A thorough understanding of a users' operating system is required for one to carry out hacking effectively. It is also necessary to have a knowledge of the operating system one intends to hack. Unlike Windows, we are able to see and even manipulate all the working parts of Linux. That is to say, Linux is completely transparent. It is not easy to understand the inner workings of a Windows operating system. The transparency aspect means working with Linux is more effective.

c) Linux distributions provide users with granular control

A Linux user has infinite control over the system i.e it is granular. This is significant when compared to a Windows operating system where a user is able to control only what Microsoft allows them to. Everything in Linux, both at the minuscule and macro level, is controlled by the terminal. Additionally, scripting is simple and effective for any scripting language in Linux.

d) Hacking resources are designed for Linux

A majority of tools used in hacking are specifically written for Linux. There are some like nmap or Metasploit that can be available for the Windows platform but still, not all their capabilities can be ported to Windows. They offer limited functionalities as compared to when they are on the Linux platform.

e) The future belongs to Linux/Unix

Over the years, you may have witnessed that Windows is slowing down and even stagnating in some departments.

Since the advent of the internet, Linux/Unix has and is still the choice operating system for web servers primarily because of its reliability, robustness, and stability. To date, almost two-thirds of web servers utilize Linux operating systems. Examples of uses of the Linux kernel are Citrix applications, Vmware, embedded systems in switches and routers, mobile devices, and so on. It has been said that the future of computing is with mobile devices including but not limited to phones and tablets. Android, which is used in most phones, is Linux while iOS is a Unix kernel. It is, therefore, difficult to see how the future is not Linux/Unix. Microsoft Windows commands a meager market share of around 7 percent. The rest of the market is either Linux or Unix. In summary, the future lies with Linux/Unix.

Using Kali Linux

This operating system, Kali Linux, was purposely meant for testing the security of a computer infrastructure so as to unearth vulnerabilities that require addressing. The following are the main steps in carrying out penetration testing on a computer network. The tools which can be used in the respective steps have also been included.

1) Reconnaissance

First and foremost, any penetration testing begins with intelligence gathering. In this stage, preliminary information about a particular target is collected. This information is what will be used in the planning of the actual attack.

Examples of tools for reconnaissance in Kali Linux are Nmap, DNSRecon, Hping3, Recon-ng among others.

2) Scanning

The second step is to scan for more intel about the target under consideration. A vulnerability scanner is employed at this step to help a penetration tester discover security loopholes that may be present in the target network.

Tools that can be used for this purpose include Nikto, Cisco-auditing-tool, WebSploit, jSQL Injection, Arp-scan, and Oscanner.

3) Gaining access

Gaining access to a targeted network is the third step. Here, an ethical hacker will make an attempt to infiltrate a network. The intention is to enable the hacker to extract vital data with which they can use to compromise a system or use it as a platform to launch more attacks.

Tools necessary for this include John the Ripper, Browser Exploitation Framework (BeEF), Metasploit Framework, Aircrack-ng, and Wireshark.

4) Maintaining access

A tester is required to maintain access to a system he or she has gained access to. This is to enable them to cause more destruction for as long as possible. To accomplish this task, stealthy tools capable of under-the-ground operations are necessary.

Some of the tools include Dns2tcp, Webshells, Powersploit, Cryptcat, and Weevely

5) Covering tracks

Here, a penetration tester will try to erase any signs or footprints of past malicious activity that has been carried out on the target network. A good example is returning original statuses of access privileges that had been escalated or altered.

Kali Linux has the following tools for covering tracks: Smbexec, Meterpreter, and Veil

Introduction to Penetration Testing

Still, on the introduction to Kali Linux, we are going to introduce penetration testing. This will give us the required background to enable us to understand its importance with regards to security analysis. Penetration testing is a valuable tool that helps security planners get to understand and improve the security of a computer or network they are managing. Nevertheless, a hacker can use penetration testing to exploit weaknesses in the system then afterward, attack them and steal valuable information. A security professional is able to use penetration testing better when he or she understands why it is needed in the first place, and also when the processes and issues surrounding it are well understood. We shall look at the terms of its use, its applications, and the various processes involved. The book is not intended to be a step-by-step guide on how to carry out penetration testing. This is a skill that requires a lot of practical practice to master. If it is not done correctly, it can actually damage the targeted or the results can be deemed invalid in some cases.

So, what is penetration testing?

We define it as an agreed set of procedures and processes that are used for bypassing laid down security controls of an intended or known system or organization purposely to test the said system's or organization's resistance capabilities against such attacks. Penetration testing is normally carried out to unearth weaknesses in the security of a system and also to find out the ways in which a systems' security architecture can be breached by a potential attacker.

Often, a penetration test comprises of a sequence of attacks against a select target. The outcome of the penetration test, successful or otherwise, is determined by the reaction of the targets to the attacks.

The determination of the ability of a target to resist or withstand an attack launched by a hostile intruder is the overall intention of carrying out this test.

Consequently, the pen-tester will utilize techniques and tricks that an actual attacker is likely to use. In other words, the tester will simulate a real-life attack against his target. This way, the tester can unearth the weak spots and improve its security way before a malicious attacker discovers them. Organizations are turning to penetration testing to help them ascertain the effectiveness of the measures they have in place to safeguard their security. During the testing process, problems might be discovered regarding the organization's security. Nevertheless, the pen-tester is required to elaborate on the 'enabling factors' that resulted in the success of the test. It is not sufficient enough for a tester to simply state that they were able to lay their hands on an organizations' sensitive data. The bonus is on the tester to give reasons why there was a lapse that enabled them to achieve their intended tasks.

A penetration test has the following basic requirements:

1) Like any other task, a penetration test needs to have a clearly defined goal or objective which is to be documented clearly. A more specific goal makes it easier to determine whether the test was a success or failure. For instance:

   Goal 1: Gain access to ABC's corporate network

   Goal 2: Gain access to ABC's corporate network through the internet and access the sales departments' file server.

   Goal 1 is not precise even though it is attainable. Goal 2 is precise and specific. This is what we are talking about.

   Every test being done requires its individual goal. If a pen-tester intends to carry out testing of more than one aspect of security in an organization, multiple other tests need to be performed. This makes it possible for a tester to easily distinguish attempts that are successful from those that are not.

2) The penetration test is time-bound. It should be performed within a limited time period exactly as it would happen in the real world. Any real-life attacker

would give up after unsuccessfully trying to penetrate a site. Additionally, the protected information being sought has a finite useful lifetime. Any penetration test needs to acknowledge this. Therefore, the goal of the test must include the time limits within which the test will be carried out based on the type of the target under consideration, the lifetime of useful information, and the level of threat that is expected.

3) The management of an organization should approve the penetration test. Since this activity will involve accessing an organizations' network and information systems, it must be authorized by the management.

Terminologies Used in Penetration Testing

Let us look at the commonly used terms associated with penetration testing. Throughout this book, we are going to use them often. They are:

- Tester: This is the entity carrying out the penetration test. It can either be a person or a group. It is a tester that plans and carries out the penetration test.

- Attacker: This is an original version of a penetration tester. The differentiating factor is that while testers intend to help improve the security of a company, an attackers' intention is malicious, i.e. to steal a company's' resources or information.

- Attack: we can say these are the attempts a hacker or a penetration tester makes to help them bypass a targets' security controls. The sequence of an attack, in most cases, has methods that are electronic, physical, or procedural.

- Management: This is an organizations' leadership. The testing process can include numerous levels of management especially those controlling specific areas. The management levels involved will have an impact with regards to the scope of the test.

- The Test Subject: This can either be a small organizational unit within a company or the entire company upon whom the penetration test will be performed.

- The target: The target is the organization or system being subjected to an attack. It can be aware of the test being done on it or not. Either way, most targets have their own safeguard mechanisms with which they can defend themselves.

Is penetration testing necessary?

First and foremost, a penetration test helps a given organization ascertain the effectiveness of the laid down security protocols. The protocols can be operational, technical or of a physical nature. A tester's job will be to determine whether these controls are up to the task by trying to overcome them. A penetration tester will also be gauging an organization's vulnerability to a specific threat. As a tester, the most crucial role is to find out how an organizations' countermeasures are effective and inform them about areas that need improvement. Also, an organization can identify threats against itself, and it is up to the tester to validate or invalidate the threats.

Often, companies use penetration tests to bolster their image to their target market. Here, a company can indicate that it was able to withstand attacks, and as such, is secure and has a robust infrastructure. This testing can also alert an organizations' management about a potential security threat existing within its operations or systems. A penetration test that is well-executed can uncover vulnerabilities systematically. The management can be unaware of the existence of these vulnerabilities.

Types of Penetration Testing

The first type examines the physical infrastructure of a subject. A tester can exploit the physical security of an organization. In most cases, the problems do not lie in the databases and other configurations, but the physical countermeasures in place. Questions to ask here include: is there adequate access control? Does the building housing the organization have security guards? Are they well trained? Is checking of sensitive materials conducted when employees exit the building? Are electronic devices registered and verified on the entry and exit of the building? To answer these questions, a tester will attempt to walk into the building at a time when people are arriving to work, say in the morning. Suppose an intruder can gain access to a company's building without being checked, they will be in a position to obtain the information they are after.

The second type of penetration testing is concerned with the operational aspects of an organization. Operational testing ascertains the effectiveness of laid down procedures of operation in the organization through circumventing those procedures. This is unlike physical testing, which only checks the physical access to networks, facilities, or company computers.

The third and final type deals with electronic testing. In this testing mechanism, a tester will attack a company's' networks, communications facilities, or computer systems. Electronic testing can be accomplished by using automated tools, or it can also be done manually. Here, the main objective is to decipher vulnerabilities to an attack by way of communications facilities and data networks that are being used by the subject under consideration.

A Tour of Kali

Once you start Kali, you'll be greeted with a login screen, as shown in Figure 1•1. Log in using the root account username root and the default password toor.

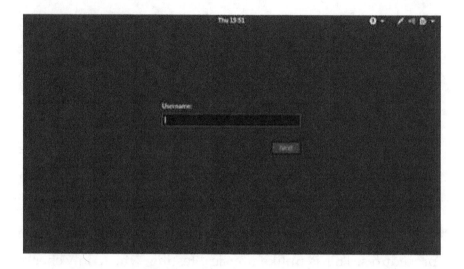

Figure: Logging into Kali using the root account

You should now have access to your Kali desktop (see Figure 1-2). We'll quickly look at two of the most basic aspects of the desktop: the terminal interface and file structure.

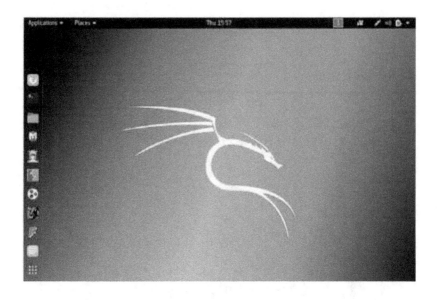

Figure: The Kali desktop

The Terminal

The first step in using Kali is to open the terminal, which is the command-line interface we'll use in this book. In Kali Linux, you'll find the icon for the terminal at the bottom of the desktop. Double•click this icon to open the terminal or press CTRL•ALT•T. Your new terminal should look like the one shown in the figure below.

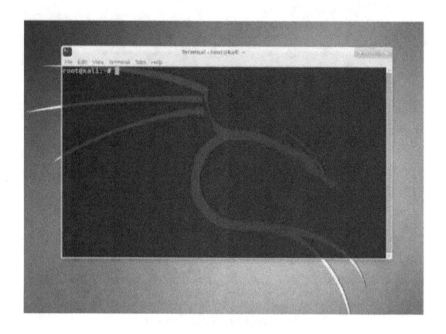

Figure: The Kali terminal

This terminal opens the command line environment, known as the shell, which enables you to run commands on the underlying operating systems and write scripts. Although Linux has many different shell environments, the most popular is the bash shell, which is also the default shell in Kali and many other Linux distributions. To change your password, you can use the command passwd.

The Linux Filesystem

The Linux filesystem structure is somewhat different from that of Windows. Linux doesn't have a physical drive (such as the C: drive) at the base of the filesystem but uses a logical filesystem instead. At the very top of the filesystem structure is /, which is often referred to as the root of the filesystem, as if it were an upside•down tree (see the figure below). Keep in mind that this is different from the root user. These terms may seem confusing at first, but they will become easier to differentiate once you get used to Linux.

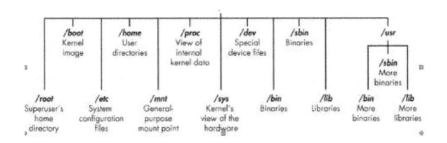

Figure: The Linux filesystem

The root (/) of the filesystem is at the top of the tree, and the following are the most important subdirectories to know:

/root: The home directory of the all•powerful root user

/etc: Generally contains the Linux configuration files — files that control when and how programs startup

/home: The user's home directory

/mnt: Where other filesystems are attached or mounted to the filesystem

/media: Where CDs and USB devices are usually attached or mounted to the filesystem

/bin: Where application binaries (the equivalent of executables in Microsoft Windows) reside

/lib: Where you'll find libraries (shared programs that are similar to Windows DLLs)

We will spend more time with these key directories throughout this book. Understanding these first•level directories is important in navigating through the filesystem from the command line.

It's also important to know before you start that you should not log in as root when performing routine tasks because anyone who hacks your system (yes, hackers sometimes get hacked) when you're logged in as root would immediately gain root privileges and thus "own" your system. Log in as a regular user when starting regular applications, browsing the web, running tools like Wireshark, and so on.

Basic Commands in Linux

To begin, let's look at some basic commands that will help you get up and running in Linux.

Finding yourself with pwd

Unlike when you're working in a graphical user interface (GUI) environment like Windows or macOS, the command line in Linux does not always make it apparent which directory you're presently in. To navigate to a new directory, you usually need to know where you are currently. The present working directory command, pwd, returns your location within the directory structure.

Enter pwdin your terminal to see where you are:

kali >pwd

/root

In this case, Linux returned /root, telling me I'm in the root user's directory. And because you logged in as root when you started Linux, you should be in the root user's directory, too, which is one level below the top of the filesystem structure (/).

If you're in another directory, pwdwill return that directory name instead.

Checking Your Login with whoami

In Linux, the one "all-powerful" superuser or system administrator is named root, and it has all the system privileges needed to add users, change passwords, change privileges, and so on. Obviously, you don't want just anyone to have the ability to make such changes; you want someone who can be trusted and has proper knowledge of the operating system. As a hacker, you usually need to have all those privileges to run the programs and commands you need (many hacker tools won't work unless you have root privileges), so you'll want to log in as root.

If you've forgotten whether you're logged in as root or another user, you can use the whoamicommand to see which user you're logged in as:

kali >whoami

root

If I had been logged in as another user, such as my personal account, whoamiwould have returned my username instead, as shown here:

kali >whoami

OTW

Navigating the Linux Filesystem

Navigating the filesystem from the terminal is an essential Linux skill. To get anything done, you need to be able to move around to find applications, files, and directories located in other directories. In a GUI•based system, you can visually see the directories, but when you're using the command-line interface, the structure is entirely text-based, and navigating the filesystem means using some commands.

Changing Directories with cd

To change directories from the terminal, use the change directory command, cd. For example, here's how to change to the /etc directory used to store configuration files:

kali   >cd/etc

root@kali:/etc#

The prompt changes to root@kali:/etc, indicating that we're in the /etc directory. We can confirm this by entering pwd:

root@kali:/etc# pwd

/etc

To move up one level in the file structure (toward the root of the file structure, or /), we use cdfollowed by double dots (..), as shown here:

root@kali:/etc# cd.

root@kali:/# pwd

/

root@kali:/#

This moves us up one level from /etc to the / root directory, but you can move up as many levels as you need. Just use the same number of double•dot pairs as the number of levels you want to move:

You would use ..to move up one level.

You would use to move up two levels.

You would use to move up three levels, and so on.

So, for example, to move up two levels, enter cdfollowed by two sets of double dots with space in between:

kali >cd....

You can also move up to the root level in the file structure from anywhere by entering cd /, where /represents the root of the filesystem.

Listing the Contents of a Directory with ls

To see the contents of a directory (the files and subdirectories), we can use the ls(list) command. This is very similar to the dircommand in Windows.

kali >ls				
bin	initrd.img	media	run	var
boot	initrd.img.old	mnt	sbin	vmlinuz
dev	lib	opt	srv	vmlinuz.old
etc	lib64	proc	tmp	
home lost+found			root	Usr

This command lists both the files and directories contained in the directory. You can also use this command on any particular directory, not just the one you are currently in, by listing the directory name after the command; for example, ls/etcshows what's in the /etc directory.

To get more information about the files and directories, such as their permissions, owner, size, and when they were last modified, you can add the -lswitch after ls(the l stands for long). This is often referred to as long listing. Let's try it here:

As you can see, ls-lprovides us with significantly more information, such as whether an object is a file or directory, the number of links, the owner, the group, its size, when it was created or modified, and its name.

I typically add the -lswitch whenever doing a listing in Linux but to each their own.

Some files in Linux are hidden and won't be revealed by a simple lsor ls-lcommand.

To show hidden files, add a lowercase –aswitch, like so:

kali >ls-la

If you aren't seeing a file you expect to see, it's worth trying lswith the aflag.

Getting Help

Nearly every command, application, or utility has a dedicated help file in Linux that provides guidance for its use. For instance, if I needed help using the best wireless cracking tool, aircrack•ng, I could simply type the aircrack-ngcommand followed by the --helpcommand:

kali >aircrack-ng--help

Note the double dash here. The convention in Linux is to use a double dash (--) before word options, such as help, and a single dash (-) before single•letter options, such as –h.

When you enter this command, you should see a short description of the tool and guidance on how to use it. In some cases, you can use either -hor -?to get to the help file.

Unfortunately, although many applications support all three options (--help, -h, and -?), there's no guarantee the application you're using will. So if one option doesn't work, try another.

Referencing Manual Pages with man

In addition to the help switch, most commands and applications have a manual (man) page with more information, such as a description and synopsis of the command or application. You can view a man page by simply typing man before the command, utility, or application. To see the man page for aircrack•ng, for example, you would enter the following:

```
kali >man aircrack-ng
NAME
       aircrack-ng - a 802.11 WEP / WPA-PSK key cracker
SYNOPSIS
       aircrack-ng [options] <.cap / .ivs file(s)>
DESCRIPTION
       aircrack-ng is an 802.11 WEP and WPA/WPA2-PSK key cracking program.
       It can recover the WEP key once enough encrypted packets have been
       captured with airodump-ng. This part of the aircrack-ng suite deter-
       mines the WEP key using two fundamental methods. The first method is
       via the PTW approach (Pyshkin, Tews, Weinmann). The main advantage
       of the PTW approach is that very few data packets are required to
       crack the WEP key. The second method is the FMS/KoreK method. The
       FMS/KoreK method incorporates various statistical attacks to dis-
       cover the WEP key and uses these in combination with brute forcing.
       Additionally, the program offers a dictionary method for determining
       the WEP key. For cracking WPA/WPA2 pre-shared keys, a wordlist (file
       or stdin) or an airolib-ng has to be used.
```

This opens the manual for aircrack•ng, providing you with more detailed information than the helpscreen. You can scroll through this manual file using the ENTER key, or you can page up and down using the PG DN and PG UP keys, respectively. To exit, simply enter q(for quit), and you'll return to the command prompt.

Finding Stuff

Until you become familiar with Linux, it can be frustrating to find your way around, but knowledge of a few basic commands and techniques will go a long way toward making the command line much friendlier. The following commands help you locate things from the terminal.

Searching with locate

Probably the easiest command to use is locate. Followed by a keyword denoting what it is you want to find, this command will go through your entire filesystem and locate every occurrence of that word.

To look for aircrack•ng, for example, enter the following:

kali >locateaircrack-ng

/usr/bin/aircrack•ng

/usr/share/applications/kali•aircrack•ng.desktop

/usr/share/desktop•directories/05•1•01•aircrack•ng.director
y

••snip••

/var/lib/dpkg/info/aircrack•ng.mg5sums

The locatecommand is not perfect, however. Sometimes, the results of locate can be overwhelming, giving you too much information. Also, locate uses a database that is usually only updated once a day, so if you just created a file a few minutes or a few hours ago, it might not appear in this list until the next day. It's worth knowing the disadvantages of these basic commands so you can better decide when best to use each one.

Finding Binaries with whereis

If you're looking for a binary file, you can use the whereiscommand to locate it. This command returns not only the location of the binary but also its source and man page if they are available. Here's an example:

kali >whereisaircrack-ng

aircarck•ng: /usr/bin/aircarck•ng
/usr/share/man/man1/aircarck•ng.1.gz

In this case, whereis returned just the aircrack•ng binaries and man page, rather than every occurrence of the word aircrack-ng. Much more efficient and illuminating, don't you think?

Finding Binaries in the PATH Variable with which

The whichcommand is even more specific: it only returns the location of the binaries in the PATHvariable in Linux. We'll look more closely at the PATHvariable in Chapter 7, but for now, it's sufficient to know that PATHholds the directories in which the operating

system looks for the commands you execute at the command line. For example, when I enter aircrack-ngon the command line, the operating system looks to the PATHvariable to see in which directories it should look for aircrack•ng:

kali >whichaircrack-ng

/usr/bin/aircrack•ng

Here, which was able to find a single binary file in the directories listed in the PATH variable. At a minimum, these directories usually include /usr/bin, but may include /usr/sbin and maybe a few others.

Performing More Powerful Searches with find

The findcommand is the most powerful and flexible of the searching utilities. It is capable of beginning your search in any designated directory and looking for a number of different parameters, including, of course, the filename but also the date of creation or modification, the owner, the group, permissions, and the size.

Here's the basic syntax for find:

find directoryoptionsexpression

So, if I wanted to search for a file with the name apache2 (the open-source webserver)

starting in the root directory, I would enter the following:

kali >find/❶ -typef❷ -nameapache2❸

First, I state the directory in which to start the search, in this case,/❶. Then I specify which type of file to search for, in this case, ffor an ordinary file ❷. Last, I give the name of the file I'm searching for, in this case, apache2❸.

My results for this search are shown here:

kali >find /-typef-nameapache2

/usr/lib/apache2/mpm•itk/apache2

/usr/lib/apache2/mpm•event/apache2

/usr/lib/apache2/mpm•worker/apache2

/usr/lib/apache2/mpm•prefork/apache2

/etc/cron.daily/apache2

/etc/logrotate.d/apache2

/etc/init.d/apache2

/etc/default/apache2

The findcommand started at the top of the filesystem (/), went through every directory looking for apache2 in the filename, and then listed all instances found.

As you might imagine, a search that looks in every directory can be slow. One way to speed it up is to look only in the directory where you would expect to find the file(s) you need. In this case, we are looking for a configuration file, so we could start the search in the /etc directory, and Linux would only search as far as its subdirectories. Let's try it:

kali >find/etc-typef-nameapache2

/etc/init.d/apache2

/etc/logrotate.d/apache2

/etc/cron.daily/apache2

This much quicker search only found occurrences of apache2 in the /etc directory and its subdirectories. It's also important to note that unlike some other search commands, finddisplays only exact name matches. If the file apache2 has an extension, such as apache2.conf, the search will not find a match. We can remedy this limitation by using wildcards, which enable us to match multiple characters. Wildcards come in a few different forms: *.,?and [].

Let's look in the /etc directory for all files that begin with apache2 and have any extension. For this, we could write a findcommand using the following wildcard:

kali>find/etc-typef
nameapache2.*/etc/apache2/apache2.conf

When we run this command, we find that there is one file in the /etc directory that fits the apache2.*pattern. When we use a period followed by the *wildcard, the terminal looks for an extension after the filename apache2. This can be a very useful technique for finding files where you don't know the file extension.

When I run this command, I find two files that start with apache2 in the /etc directory, including the apache2.conf file.

Chapter : 3
Hardware Hacking Using Linux

As you begin your journey towards being a hacker, you will realize that most of the professional and expert hackers make use of Linux/Unix in their trade. That aside, we have some types of hacks where Mac OS and Windows can be used. Software such as Zenmap, Metasploit, Havij, Cain, and Abel and others have Windows versions. Usually, when the applications are developed in Linux and later ported to Windows, they always lose some of their capabilities. That is to say; we have capabilities that are found in Linux but are not present in Windows. This is the reason that many hacker tools are designed and build for Linux. It is, therefore, essential that anyone who intends to be a professional hacker learns or has some basics of a Linux distribution like Kali.

Why Hackers use Linux

Below are some of the main reasons why hackers prefer Linux.

1) Linux is Open Source

Unlike the Windows operating system software, Linux distribution is an open source. A Linux user has access to the operating systems' source code. This means that one can manipulate and change a Linux operating system to suit their needs at will. Supposing the user wants to make a particular system operate in ways besides those it was originally intended to, the ability to manipulate and change the source code is of paramount importance.

2) Linux is Transparent

A thorough understanding of a users' operating system is required for one to carry out hacking effectively. It is also necessary to have a knowledge of the operating system one intends to hack. Unlike Windows, we can see and even manipulate all the working parts of Linux. That is to say, Linux is entirely transparent. It is not easy to understand the inner workings of a Windows operating system. The transparency aspect means working with Linux is more effective.

3) Linux Offers Granular Control

A Linux user has infinite control over the system, i.e., it is granular. This is significant when compared to a Windows operating system where a user can control only what Microsoft allows them to. Everything in Linux, both at the minuscule and macro level, is controlled by the terminal. Additionally, scripting is simple and effective for any scripting language in Linux.

4) Most Hacking Tools are Written for Linux

A majority of tools used in hacking are written explicitly for Linux. There are some like Nmap or Metasploit that can be available for the Windows platform but still, not all their capabilities can be ported to Windows. They offer limited functionalities as compared to when they are on the Linux platform.

5) The Future Belongs to Linux/Unix

Over the years, you may have witnessed that Windows is slowing down and even stagnating in some departments. Since the advent of the internet, Linux/Unix has and is still the choice operating system for web servers primarily because of its reliability, robustness, and stability. To date, almost two-thirds of web servers utilize Linux operating systems. Examples of uses of the Linux kernel are Citrix applications, Vmware, embedded systems in switches and routers, mobile devices, and so on. It has been said that the future of computing is with mobile devices including but not limited to phones and tablets. Android, which is used in most phones, is Linux while iOS is a Unix kernel. It is, therefore, difficult to see how the future is not Linux/Unix. Microsoft Windows commands a meager market share of around 7 percent. The rest of the market is either Linux or Unix. In summary, the future lies with Linux/Unix.

What is Kali Linux?

Kali Linux is a distribution of the Debian family. It was designed and developed solely for Security Auditing and Penetration Testing. The distro comprises hundreds of tools and utilities that are focussed on information security tasks which may include Reverse Engineering, Penetration Testing, Computer Forensics, and Security research. Offensive Security is the information security organization behind Kali Linux. It developed funds and maintains Kali Linux.

This distribution was initially launched in March 2013 to be a total rebuild of BackTrack Linux, top to bottom. It adhered to Debian development standards a hundred percent. Kali Linux

51

boasts of over 600 tools that can be used for penetration testing. After a thorough review of BackTrack Linux, some tools that did not work or were in duplicate were eliminated. From the Kali Tools site, lets us look at some of the details:

Kali Linux will always be free: Just like BackTrack, kali is free of charge and always will be. This implies that you are not going to pay for it at any time now or in the future.

It is Open source: The source code Kali Linux uses is available to everyone that wants to improve, modify, or rebuild packages to adapt them to their specific requirements.

Kali complies with FHS: The distribution follows the Filesystem Hierarchy Standard. The standards help the users of Linux to locate support files, binaries, libraries, and so on seamlessly.

Support a wide range of wireless devices: The system has been designed with multiple platforms to support wireless interfaces. It can run on a wide range of hardware

The kernel is customized and is patched for injection: Latest injection patches are included in the Kali Linux kernel.

It was created in an environment that is secure: The team tasked with the development of Kali is a small group of individuals that are trusted to commit packages and interact with the repositories. Secure protocols are used in these processes.

GPG signed repositories and packages: All packages in Kali Linux are usually signed by the individual developers. It is these developers that are responsible for the packages. The packages are subsequently signed by the repositories as well.

Support for Multiple languages: Most penetration tools and utilities are often written in English. Kali, notwithstanding, offers true multilingual support. Users are, therefore, able to operate in their native languages. Isn't that a great thing!

Kali is easily customizable: All users can modify Kali to their requirements and preferences.

Downloading Kali Linux

Before I take you down the road towards being a hacker, you will first be required to download and install Kali Linux on your computer. This is the distribution of Linux that we shall be using throughout this book. That can be done from https://www.kali.org/. Navigate to the home page and hit the Downloads link located at the top of the page. It is important that the right download is selected.

The Procedure for Installing Kali and Setting Up Kali Linux

To start us off, you will need to boot using your preferred medium of installation. You should be greeted with the Kali Boot screen, as shown below. Choose either Text-Mode or Graphical install. In this example, we chose a GUI install.

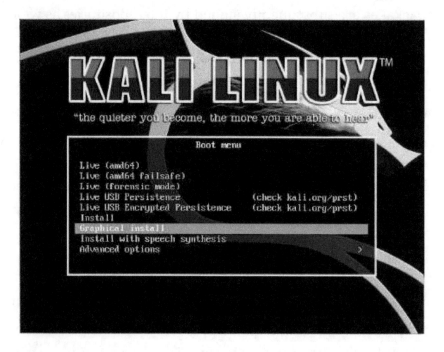

Choose your language preference together with your country location. Also, you will be prompted to select your preferred keyboard layout.

Select your location, geographic that is.

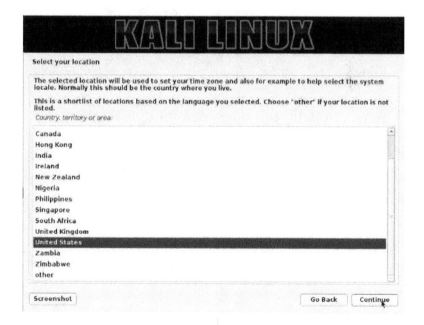

The installer will copy the image to your hard disk, probe your network interfaces, and then prompt you to enter a hostname for your system. In the example below, we've entered "kali" as our hostname.

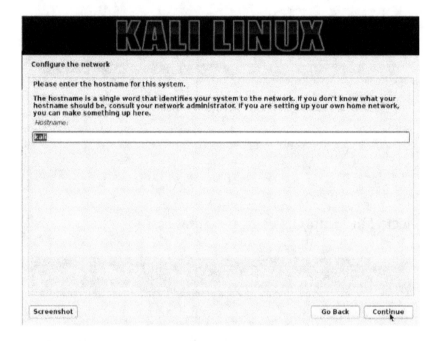

You may optionally provide a default domain name for this system to use.

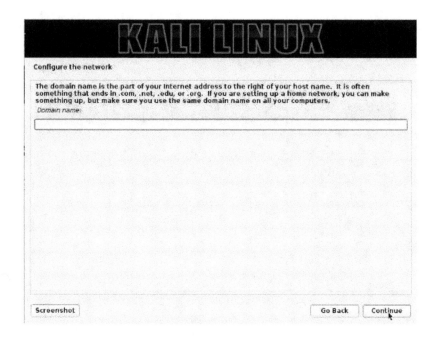

Next, provide a full name for a non-root user for the system.

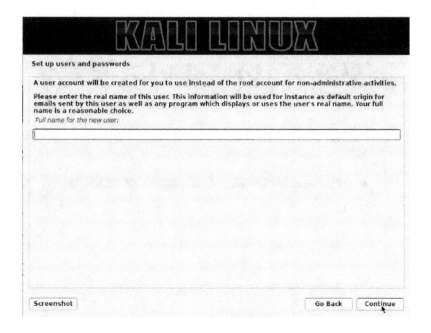

A default user ID will be created, based on the full name you provided. You can change this if you like.

After that, pick an appropriate time zone.

Next, you will see something similar to the picture below.
Select appropriately.

Choose the disk you want to be partitioned.

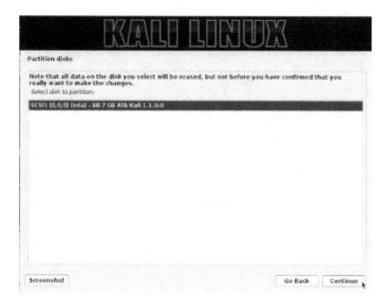

Continue to the next step below, selecting a choice depending on your needs.

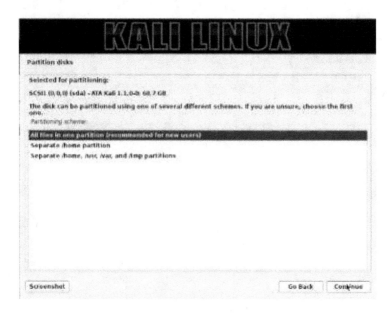

Next, hit the Continue button.

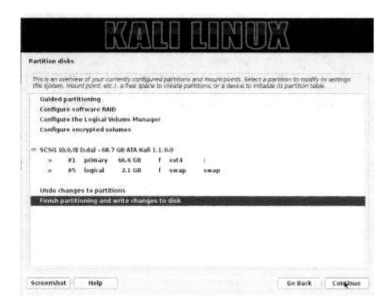

The next step requires you to carry out a configuration of network mirrors.

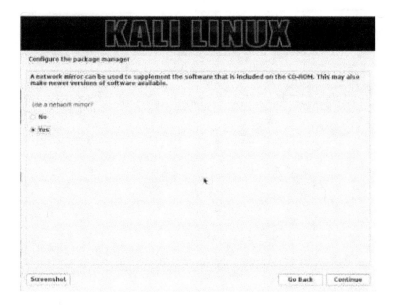

Next, install GRUB.

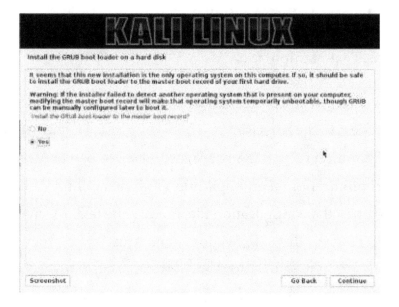

Finally, click Continue to reboot into your new Kali installation.

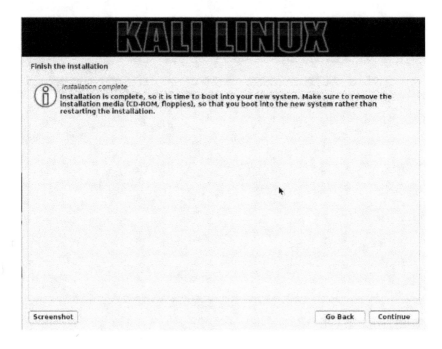

Text Manipulation and Bash Scripting

A. Text manipulation

As we have seen before, almost everything in Linux is a file, text files to be precise. A good example is that all the configuration files in Linux are text files. For one to carry out a reconfiguration of an application in Linux, all they need to do is open the configuration file, modify the text, re-save, and then restart the application, and just like that, the reconfiguration will be applied. Manipulation of text becomes of essence in managing Linux applications given the numerous text files. Let us look at a number of commands and techniques that are used to manipulating texts in Linux. I am going to use files from Snort for demonstration purposes.

Step 1: Cat Command

Cat is the most basic text display command. Let us cat the Snort config file that is normally found in /etc/snort.

kali > cat /etc/snort/snort.conf

From above, you can see that snort.conf is displayed on our screen until it comes to the end of the file. Definitely, that is not a convenient method to work with the file.

Step 2: Use the Head Command

We can use the head command supposing we just want to view the beginning of a file. By default, this command displays a files' beginning 10 lines.

kali > head /etc/snort/snort.conf

In cases where we want to view more or fewer lines, we can use the "- switch" between the command and the file name.

kali > head -15 /etc/snort/snort.conf

Here, only the first 15 lines of snort.conf will be displayed.

Step 3: Tail Command

Just like the head command, we can see the last lines of a file by using this command. The syntax of the command is as below:

kali > tail -20 /etc/snort/snort.conf

Step 4: Numbering The Lines

With long files, it may be desirable to display them with line numbers. snort.conf, for instance, has over 600 lines. Numbering makes it a lot easier for referencing changes, and also, it is easy to come back to the same place within a file. To show a file with a line number, we type:

kali > nl /etc/snort/snort.conf

Each line will now have a number making referencing much easier.

Step 5: Grep Command

Grep is a filtering command, that is, it gives us a chance to filter the content of a file for display. Grep is an essential and powerful command for working in Linux since it can minimize wastage of time spent in searching for every occurrence of a word or command.

Step 6: Sed Command

This command enables us to look up for occurrences of a word or text pattern and then work on it. The name is a contraction of two words, stream and editor. Simply put, sed works in the same way as the find and replace function in Windows.

Step 7: Less and More Commands

Like we have previously said, cat is a good utility command. However, it has a number of shortcomings where the display of large files is involved. Remember us saying cat is not very convenient?

More came first and is the utility that manual pages use. Let's open snort.conf with more command.

kali > more /etc/snort/snort.conf

You will see that more displays only the first page and displays for us in the lower-left corner how much of the file is being shown. Less is similar to more, although it possesses some additional functionality. To open snort.conf with less, type the following:

kali > less /etc/snort/snort.conf

You will see near the bottom left of the screen that less has highlighted the path to the file.

B. Bash Scripting

A bash script can be described as a file consisting of plain text having a sequence of commands. The commands include those that we can type normally into the command line on our own and those we generally wouldn't type. Take note of this: Any command that is able to be executed normally from the Kali Linux terminal may be placed in the bash script. The reverse is also true. Nothing needs changing. The commands just need to be typed normally, and they will behave as they are supposed to. Let me put it this way, suppose you are familiar with the Kali command line, you will be able to carry out bash scripting as they are almost similar. Normally, an extension of .sh is affixed to all the scripts in Bash. This is, however, not necessary as the Linux system is extensionless. A script can just work fine without this feature.

How do these scripts work?

If you have been interacting with computers generally, you appreciate that we have things we call programs and others that we call processes. We all agree that a program comprises a sequence of instructions made for the computer's central processing unit combined into a package and usually stored on the computers' hard disk.

When a program runs, what is actually running is its copy. This copy is referred to as a process. What is being done here is that the instructions alongside other relevant resources are being copied to the RAM (that is, the working memory) form the hard disk. Also, temporary storage space in the RAM is allocated for temporary data and flags which will be used by the operating system to track and manage the process as it executes. Ideally, a process is a running instance of a program.

In normal circumstances, we have several processes that represent a single program running in the computers' memory all at the same time. Upon their completion, the system will destroy them so that we will not have any more processes for the program. At the terminal, we will be having a running Bash process to provide us the Bash shell.

How does the bash script run?

This is quite easy. First, running a script is also known as executing a script.

We have to set permissions to execute scripts. These permissions for safety reasons are by default, not set. Skipping this step will only display an error message but the code can still run. Let's look at a sample script below.

1. *#!/bin/bash*

2. *# This is an example of a Bash script, by Sutherland*

3.

4. *echo Welcome to Kali Linux!*

We are going to expound a little bit on what is going on here below:

- Line no. 1 – That as what we call the shebang.
- Line no. 2 - This is a comment. Anything after # is not executed.
- Line no. 4 - Is the command echo which will print a message to the screen. On Line no. 2, you will see that it is highlighted. Highlighting the syntax only serves to make it easy to read. You probably do not need it in your own files.

What is the use of ./

For normal commands, all we need to do is type the name and voila! It starts to execute. To run a bash script, we place ./ in front of it. Bash will attempt to find the name you have typed on the command line without ./ in directories that are located in a variable called $PATH. Separation of the directories is done using " : " This script will perform a search in those particular directories and will not look at your current directory or other subdirectories.

Bash will run the first instance of the script or program that it finds after searching the directories mentioned above. It is prudent to note that the $PATH variable varies with each individual user and they can set it up to their preference.

Below are the reasons that this is done:

1   This way, we can install a number of different versions of a particular program. We are also able to determine which of them gets executed depending on their location in $PATH.

2   It offers unprecedented convenience. From the lengthy explanation above, the bin directory is found on the home directory. A user is in a position to place their own programs and installed scripts in there. A user is also able to utilize them regardless of their location within the system just by doing a simple name typing. It is also possible to make scripts with a similar name as a program in case you desire to have a behavior that is slightly different.

3   The overall safety is increased – look at this, a malicious user may make a script intended to delete everything from the home directory. It is in your best interest not to execute that script. As long as the script is not in your $PATH, no problems will arise.

You are also able to tell bash where to find a program script suppose it does not lie in any of the directories in your $PATH. This can be done by including a relative or an absolute path in front of the script name or program. Do not forget that the dot (.) refers to the current directory you are in. Supposing the script is situated in the home directory, you can execute it through the use of an absolute path.

The Shebang (#!)

From the script above, we can see that this is found in the first line.

The character sequence of hash and exclamation mark (#!) is what is called the Shebang. What follows the shebang is a path to the program or interpreter which does the execution of the remainder of the text file. It is essential that we get the formatting right here. Shebang must be placed at the files' very first line. Let me repeat, the #! Has to be inserted at line 1 of the file. One other thing to pay attention to is that there should be no spaces between the sign # , the mark ! and the interpreter path. It is unwise to also omit the shebang since the Bash shell will make an assumption that it is a Bash script. This means that it will work only by the assumption that the script is being run in a Bash shell which is not entirely true. That is a very dangerous scenario.

Bash scripts formatting

Formatting is an important area of bash scripting required in many areas to enable the proper functioning of the scripts. Absence or presence of a space between commands can make it either work or refuse to work. It is paramount that you familiarize yourself with this issue in your coding exercise. This type of scripting was purposely designed to act as an interface through which users are able to interact with the system. Later on, the capabilities of bash as a scripting tool continued to become advanced. The improvements were initially made based on user needs then the scripting capabilities were worked around the various user needs. I know it can be annoying for a finely written piece of code to fail. Another formatting requirement is the indentation of code. You may already know by now that it is not required for a given code to run, but its role is to ensure the readability of the code. It also makes it easier to keep the simple mistakes at bay.

Chapter : 4
Network Security

Nearly everything we do on the internet is tracked. Whoever is doing the tracking, whether it be Google tracking our online searches, website visits, and email or the National Security Agency (NSA) cataloging all our activities, all our online moves are being recorded, indexed, and then mined for someone's benefit. The average individual and the hacker, in particular, need to understand how to limit this tracking and remain relatively anonymous on the web to limit this ubiquitous surveillance. In this chapter, we look at how you can navigate the World Wide Web anonymously (or as close as you can get) using four methods:

- The Onion Network
- Proxy servers
- Virtual private networks
- Private encrypted email

No one method is sure to keep your activities safe from prying eyes, and given enough time and resources; anything can be tracked. However, these methods will likely make the tracker's job much more difficult.

How the Internet gives us away

To begin, let's discuss, at a high level, some of the ways our activities on the internet are tracked. We won't go into all tracking methods or into too much detail about any one process as that would be beyond the scope of this book. Indeed, such a discussion could take up an entire book on its own. First, your IP address identifies you as you traverse the internet. Data sent from your machine is generally tagged with your IP address, making your activities easy to track.

Second, Google and other email services will "read" your email, looking for keywords to more efficiently serve your ads. Although there are many more sophisticated methods that are far more time and resource-intensive, these are the ones we try to prevent in this chapter. Let's start by taking a look at how IP addresses give us away on the internet.

When you send a packet of data across the internet, it contains the IP addresses of the source and destination for the data. In this way, the packet knows where it is going and where to return the response. Each packet hops through multiple internet routers until it finds its destination and then jumps back to the sender. For general internet surfing, each hop is a router the packet passes through to get to its destination. There can be as many as 20–30 hops between the sender and the destination, but usually, any packet will find its way to the destination in fewer than 15 hops.

As the packet traverses the internet, anyone intercepting the packet can see who sent it, where it has been, and where it is going. This is one way websites can tell who you are when you arrive and log you in automatically, and it is also how someone can track where you've been on the internet. To see what hops a packet might make between you and the destination, you can use the traceroute command, as shown next. Enter traceroute and the destination IP address or domain, and the command will send out packets to the destination and trace the route of those packets.

The Onion Router System

In the 1990s, the US Office of Naval Research (ONR) set out to develop a method for anonymously navigating the internet for espionage purposes. The plan was to set up a network of routers that was separate from the internet's routers that could encrypt the traffic and that only stored the unencrypted IP address of the previous router — meaning all other router addresses along the way were encrypted. The idea was that anyone watching the traffic could not determine the origin or destination of the data. This research became known as "The Onion Router (Tor) Project" in 2002, and it's now available to anyone to use for relatively safe and anonymous navigation on the web.

How Tor Works

Packets sent over Tor are generally not sent over the regular routers so closely monitored by so many but instead are sent over a network of over 7,000 routers around the world, thanks to volunteers who allow their computers to be utilized by Tor. On top of using an entirely separate router network, Tor encrypts the data, destination, and sender IP address of each packet. At each hop, the information is encrypted and then decrypted by the next hop when it's received. In this way, each packet contains information about only the previous hop along the path and not the IP address of the origin. If someone intercepts the traffic, they can see only the IP address of the previous hop, and the website owner can see only the IP address of the last router that sent the traffic.

This ensures relative anonymity across the internet. To enable the use of Tor, you need to install the Tor browser from https://www.torproject.org/. Once installed, you can use it like any old internet browser. By using this browser, you will be navigating the internet through a separate set of routers and will be able to visit sites without being tracked by Big Brother. Unfortunately, the tradeoff is that surfing via the Tor browser can be a lot slower; because there are not nearly as many routers, the bandwidth is limited in this network.

In addition to being capable of accessing nearly any website on the traditional internet, the Tor browser is capable of accessing the dark web. The sites that make up the dark web require anonymity, so they allow access only through the Tor browser, and they have addresses ending in .onion for their top level domain (TLD). The dark web is infamous for illegal activity, but there exist quite a number of legal services that are also available there. A word of caution, however: when accessing the dark web, you may come across material that many will find offensive.

Security Concerns

The intelligence and spy services of the United States and other nations consider the Tor network a threat to national security, believing such an anonymous network enables foreign governments and terrorists to communicate without being watched. As a result, we have numerous robust and ambitious research projects are working to break the anonymity of Tor. Tor's anonymity has been broken before by these authorities and will likely be broken again. The NSA, as one instance, runs its own Tor routers, meaning that your traffic may be traversing the NSA's routers when you use Tor.

If your traffic is exiting the NSA's routers, that's even worse, because the exit router always knows your destination. The NSA also has a method known as traffic correlation, which involves looking for patterns in incoming and outgoing traffic, that has been able to break Tor's anonymity. Though these attempts to break Tor won't affect Tor's effectiveness at obscuring your identity from commercial services, such as Google, they may limit the browser's effectiveness in keeping you anonymous from spy agencies.

Proxy Servers

Another strategy for achieving anonymity on the internet is to use proxies, which are intermediate systems that act as middlemen for traffic: the user connects to a proxy, and the traffic is given the IP address of the proxy before it's passed on.

When the traffic returns from the destination, the proxy sends the traffic back to the source. In this way, traffic appears to come from the proxy and not the originating IP address. Most probably, the proxy will keep a log of your traffic. However, an investigating entity would need to obtain a search warrant or subpoena in order for them to obtain the logs. To make your traffic even harder to trace, you can use more than one proxy, in a strategy known as a proxy chain, which we'll look at a little later in this chapter. Kali Linux has an excellent proxying tool called proxychains that you can set up to obscure your traffic. The syntax for the proxychains command is straightforward, as shown here:

kali >proxychains <the command you want proxied> <arguments>

The arguments you provide might include an IP address.

Setting Proxies in the Config File

In this section, we set a proxy for the proxychains command to use. As with nearly every application in Linux/Unix, the configuration of proxychains is managed by the config file — specifically /etc/proxychains.conf. Open the config file in your text editor of choice with the following command (replacing leafpad with your chosen editor if necessary):

kali >leafpad /etc/proxychains.conf

You should see a proxychains.conf file. Scroll down this file to line 61, and you should see the ProxyList section. We can add proxies by entering the IP addresses and ports of the proxies we want to use in this list.

Security Concerns

As a last note on proxy security, be sure to choose your proxies wisely: proxychains is only as good as the proxies you use. If you are intent on remaining anonymous, do not use a free proxy, as mentioned earlier. Hackers use paid for proxies that can be trusted. The free proxies are likely selling your IP address and browsing history. As Bruce Schneier, the famous cryptographer and security expert, once said, "If something is free, you're not the customer; you're the product." In other words, any free product is likely gathering your data and selling it. Why else would they offer a proxy for free? Although the IP address of your traffic leaving the proxy will be anonymous, there are other ways for surveillance agencies to identify you. For instance, the owner of the proxy will know your identity and, if pressured enough by espionage or law enforcement agencies with jurisdiction, may offer up your identity to protect their business. It is good to be aware of the limitations of proxies as a source of anonymity.

Virtual Private Networks

Using a virtual private network can be an effective way to keep your web traffic relatively anonymous and secure. A VPN is used to connect to an intermediary internet device such as a router that sends your traffic to its ultimate destination tagged with the IP address of the router. Using a VPN can certainly enhance your security and privacy, but it is not a guarantee of anonymity. The internet device you connect to must record or log your IP address to be able to send the data back to you accurately, so anyone able to access these records can uncover information about you.

The beauty of VPNs is that they are simple and easy to work with. You can open an account with a VPN provider and then seamlessly connect to the VPN each time you log on to your computer. You would use your browser as usual to navigate the web, but it will appear to anyone watching that your traffic is coming from the IP address and location of the internet VPN device and not your own. Besides, all traffic between you and the VPN device is encrypted, so even your internet service provider cannot see your traffic.

Among other things, a VPN can be useful in evading government-controlled Content and information censors. For instance, if your national government limits your access to websites with particular political messages, you can likely use a VPN based outside your country to access that Content. Some media corporations, such as Netflix, limit access to their Content to IP addresses originating from their nation. Using a VPN based in a country that those services allow can often get you around those access limitations. Some of the best VPN services are: IPVanish, NordVPN, ExpressVPN, CyberGhost, Golden Frog VPN, Hide My Ass, Private Internet Access, PureVPN, TorGuard, and Buffered VPN

The strength of a VPN is that all your traffic is encrypted when it leaves your computer, thus protecting you against snooping, and your IP address is cloaked by the VPN IP address when you visit a site. As with a proxy server, the owner of the VPN has your originating IP address.

Ipsec

IPsec is used to provide data integrity, authentication, and confidentiality between two points across the IP network that are in communication. It is an Internet Engineering Task Force protocol that also provides definitions of the encrypted, decrypted and authenticated packets. Additionally, key management and secure key exchange protocols are defined in IPsec.

Functions of IP Security

The following are tasks that can be done by IPsec:

- For encryption of data found in the application layer.

- Securing routers transmitting data over the internet.

- IPsec provides us with authentication without there being any encryption.

- It does the safeguarding of data on the network through the creation of circuits using IPsec tunneling. This works just like the Virtual Private Network.

IP Security Components

Below are some of the components that comprise an IPsec:

i. **Internet Key Exchange (IKE)** – This is a protocol for network security that has been designed to exchange encryption keys dynamically as well as bypass the Security Association (SA) between two devices. SA is used for the establishment of security attributes that are shared between any two network elements. These attributes are what support secure communications. Additionally, IKE offers protection to contents of messages plus an open frame that can be used for the implementation of standard algorithms, for instance, MD5 and SHA.

ii. **Encapsulating Security Payload (ESP)** – This is used to ensure data integrity, authentication, anti-replay, and encryption. ESP also does payload authentication.

iii.   **Authentication Header (AH)** – IPsec uses an authentication header to ensure there is data integrity, anti-replay, and authentication. An authentication header, however, does not offer encryption. The anti-replay protection function is used to guard against unauthorized packet transmission, but it does not keep the data confidential.

The Operation of IP Security

1   First, a host will check to see if a packet needs to be send using IPsec or not. It is the traffic of the packets that trigger the security policy on their own.

2   Phase 1 of the internet key exchange begins with the two hosts that are utilizing IPsec authenticating themselves to each other. That will start a secure channel. Here, we have two modes:

- The Main mode which is used for the provision of the greater security and;

- The Aggressive mode that makes a host be able to create an IPsec circuit expeditiously.

3   Using the above channel (established in step 2), negotiation on the manner in which the IP circuit will encrypt data across the IP circuit will be done.

4   After that, the Phase 2 internet key exchange happens over the secure channel that was negotiated.

5   Data exchanged is then carried out over the newly established IPsec encrypted tunnel. Encryption and decryption of packets are carried out by the hosts through IPsec SAs.

6   Upon the completion of communication, or time-out of a session between the hosts, the IPsec tunnel will be terminated. Both the hosts will discard the keys

Chapter : 5
Social Engineering

Social engineering is increasingly becoming a major threat to virtual entities and is also becoming an effective vector with which to attack information systems. Most services in use today lay a good foundation for sophisticated social engineering attacks. In every major institution worldwide, the trend is towards bringing your own device to the workplaces, schools and social places. That may appear an effective way of enabling communication and collaboration in environments that are private or business in nature. This policy has aggravated this problem to a terrifying extent.

Global organizations are no longer staffing geographically but rather use a just-in-time strategy to cater to their staffing demands. Consequently, we have seen personal interaction decreasing as it is being replaced by a plethora of tools that have bridged the communication gap. These tools can be e-mail, Skype, and many more. All this has resulted in new vectors of attack for social engineering attacks. When social engineering attacks are combined together with zero-day-exploits, they have the potential to be a deadly weapon. This mechanism is what is commonly used by APTs, that is, advanced persistent threats.

What is Social Engineering?

We define social engineering as a broad range of activities that are malicious in nature that is accomplished via human interactions. This type of attack employs the use of psychological manipulation for purposes of tricking the users into giving away sensitive information or making security-related mistakes. Usually, social engineering attacks are carried out in a number of steps.

As usual, a perpetrator will initially carry out a reconnaissance on the intended victim to enable them to collect necessary information on their background. That background information may include identification of potential entry points and weak security protocols. This step is essential as it will dictate how the attack will proceed. Thereafter, an attacker will speedily move to win the victim's trust plus offer appealing incentives for subsequent actions that go against the laid down security practices, like exposing information that is sensitive or granting access to resources that are critical. These attacks are deadly due to their reliance on errors committed by humans instead of the vulnerabilities in the operating systems or the software. The human-made mistakes have a characteristic of being less predictable, thus making them difficult to pinpoint and guard against as compared to an intrusion that is malware-based.

Techniques for Attacks used by Social engineering

These types of attacks can be in multiple and different forms. As long as there is human interaction is involved, a social engineering attack can be carried out. Let us look at the following five commonly perpetrated social engineering attacks.

- **Pretexting**

An attacker will attempt to gain access to information by a sequence of cleverly crafted lies. Pretexting is in most cases started by a perpetrator pretending that they require some crucial information from an unsuspecting victim to do a task that is critical. The attacker commences by building or winning the trust of their victim by impersonating police, bank officials, tax officials, co-workers or any other person with a right-to-know authority. The pretexter will then ask questions that will require a user to confirm their identity. This way, an attacker is able to collect critical personal data.

- **Phishing**

Popular phishing scams are in the form of text message and email campaigns that are meant to create a feeling of curiosity, compelling urgency or even instill fear in potential casualties. The victims are then prodded into disclosing information that is deemed sensitive, following the links to malicious websites by clicking on them, or by downloading and opening unknown attachments containing malware. For instance, users of a particular online service can send an email to alerts them of a policy violation that requires an action to be done immediately on their part. An example of such an action is a password change. Upon clicking the link, the user will be redirected to an illegitimate website that is almost identical in every aspect as the legitimate one, prompting an unsuspecting user to input his/her credentials to the website. That information is sent to the attacker once the form is submitted.

- **Baiting**

This type of attack utilizes a false promise to capitalize on a victim's curiosity or greed, mostly greed. Users are lured into a trap which leads to stealing their personal information. Also, malware can be sent to their systems this way. The most reviled form of baiting uses physical media to disperse malware. For instance, attackers leave the bait, typically malware-infected flash drives, in areas where potential victims are likely to see them. The bait has an authentic look to it. Victims who are unsuspecting will take up the bait due to curiosity. Afterward, they are likely to insert the device into a computer either at work or at home. This will lead to the automatic installation of malware on the system. This type of attack can be carried out in the physical or online world.

- **Scareware**

This strategy of attack involves bombarding the victims with numerous false alarms or fictitious threats. Gullible users will be tricked into thinking their system has become malware-infected. This will cause them to install software with no actual benefit or even install the malware itself. An example of scareware is "Your computer is infected by a harmful program" banner. Also, scareware is able to be spread via spam email issuing bogus warnings or offering users a chance to purchase worthless and harmful services.

- **Spear phishing**

Since we now know what phishing is, let us look at spear phishing. Here, an attacker targets specific enterprises or individuals. After identifying a target, they will go ahead and tailor-make their messages factoring issues such as job positions, contacts, and characteristics that can be attributed to their targets so as to make the attack less conspicuous. This type of phishing attack needs a lot of effort from an attacker and usually takes a very long time to pull it off successfully. Such attacks have impressive success rates when they are executed skillfully. They are also more difficult to detect.

Social engineering prevention

When it comes to social engineering, the perpetrators carry out manipulation of human sentiments, which include fear or curiosity, so that they are able to affect their malicious schemes thereby luring victims into their traps. It is paramount that we be vigilant at all times if we are to keep social engineering attacks at bay. Let us look at tips that can help us deal with this type of attack below.

Update your antivirus software –engaged automatic updates on your devices. Ensure that you download the latest signatures for your protection software frequently, say every day. Carry out a periodic check to ascertain that the updates you have downloaded have been applied. It goes without saying that you need to scan your system for possible infections.

Adopt a multifactor authentication – this means that in the unfortunate event that your systems are compromised, all your accounts will still be safeguarded. This is because one of the most valuable pieces of information attackers seek are user credentials.

Stop accepting of suspect offers – think twice before accepting an offer that sounds too good to be true. A simple google search on the topic can come in handy to enable you to help you judge if you are being lured into a trap or whether what you have with you is a legitimate offer.

Don't open suspicious emails/attachments – When you receive an email from an unknown sender who looks suspicious, do not open it. If the sender in question is known, you may want to crosscheck from them or other sources in cases where it is a company email. You can use a telephone to call for verification. Alternatively, you may opt to get details directly from the provider of the service. As you may have learned now, it is possible to spoof email addresses. That means that an attacker is able to impersonate a genuine email. Never take a chance.

Chapter : 6
Network Scanning and Management

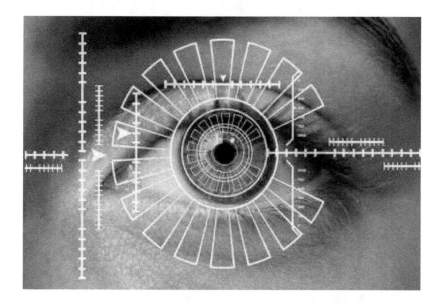

The ability to scan for and connect to other network devices from your system is crucial to becoming a successful hacker, and with wireless technologies like WiFi

and Bluetooth becoming the standard, finding and controlling WiFi and Bluetooth connections is vital. If someone can hack a wireless connection, they can gain entry to a device and access to confidential information. The first step, of course, is to learn how to find these devices. In this chapter, we are going to examine two of the most common wireless technologies in Linux: WiFi and Bluetooth.

Network Scanning

We say that it is the utilization of a computer network for purposes of collecting information about IT systems. We carry out scanning of networks primarily to help us do system maintenance or a security assessment. Hackers can also conduct a network scanning exercise before launching their attacks. The following are some of the reasons we scan networks:

- Identification of the available UDP and TCP network services that may be running on the targets.
- To get to understand the systems for filtering that are in between the targeted hosts and the user.
- Discover the operating systems that are being used through the assessment of their IP responses.
- Analyze a particular host that is being targeted for its TCP sequence number predictability to enable the prediction of TCP spoofing and the attack sequence.

Network scanning comprises of two key aspects: Vulnerability scanning and network port scanning. The latter denotes a way of sending data packets through a network over to a systems' specific port numbers. The goal is to discover network services that are present in that particular system. It is an excellent way for troubleshooting issues that a given system has. That way, the problems can be dealt with so that the system is secure. For us to discover known vulnerabilities present in network systems, a method known as vulnerability scanning is used. Through it, we can identify weak spots both in the operating system and the application software. It is these weak points that are usually used to compromise computing systems.

Both vulnerability scanning and network port scanning can be said to be techniques that are used in information gathering. On the flip side, they can be a prelude to an attack when they are put to use by anonymous entities. Such entities usually have malicious intentions. The inverse mapping is another technique for network scanning. It is useful when it comes to collecting IP addresses that are not mapped to live hosts. By doing so, it will be aiding in the focussing attention on addresses that are worth focussing on, that is, those that are feasible. There are three stages in which information gathering can be accomplished.

i.   The footprinting stage,
ii. The scanning stage, and
iii. The enumeration stage.

This, therefore, implies that network scanning is among the crucial steps an attacker needs to be able to gather information.

Network scanning with ifconfig

The ifconfig command is one of the essential tools that can be used for examining and interacting with active network interfaces. You can use it to query your active network connections by simply entering ifconfig in the terminal.

Scanning Wireless Networks with iwconfig

If you have a wireless adapter, you can use the iwconfig command to gather crucial information for wireless hacking such as the adapter's IP address, its MAC address, what mode it's in, and more. The information you can glean from this command is particularly important when you're using wireless hacking tools like aircrackng.

Changing your network information

Being able to change your IP address and other network information is a useful skill because it will help you access other networks while appearing as a trusted device on those networks. For example, in a denial of service (DoS) attack, you can spoof your IP so that that the attack appears to come from another source, thus helping you evade IP capture during forensic analysis. This is a relatively simple task in Linux, and it's done with the ifconfig command.

Changing Your IP Address

To change your IP address, enter ifconfig followed by the interface you want to reassign and the new IP address you want to be assigned to that interface. For example, to assign the IP address 192.168.181.115 to interface eth0, you would enter the following:

Kali >ifconfig eth0 192.168.181.115

kali >

When you do this correctly, Linux will go back to the command prompt and say nothing. This is a good thing! Then, when you again check your network connections with ifconfig, you should see that your IP address has changed to the new IP address you just assigned.

Changing Your Network Mask and Broadcast Address

You can also change your network mask (netmask) and broadcast address with the ifconfig command. For instance, if you want to assign that same eth0 interface with a netmask of 255.255.0.0 and a broadcast address of 192.168.1.255, you would enter the following:

Kali >ifconfig eth0 192.168.181.115 netmask 255.255.0.0 broadcast

192.168.1.255

kali >

Once again, if you've done everything correctly, Linux responds with a new command prompt. Now enter ifconfig again to verify that each of the parameters has been changed accordingly.

Spoofing Your MAC Address

You can also use ifconfig to change your MAC address. The MAC address is globally unique and is often used as a security measure to keep hackers out of networks — or to trace them. Changing your MAC address to spoof a different MAC address is almost trivial and neutralizes those security measures. Thus, it's an instrumental technique for bypassing network access controls. To spoof your MAC address, use the ifconfig command's down option to take down the interface (eth0 in this case). Then enter the ifconfig command followed by the interface name (hw for hardware, ether for Ethernet) and the new spoofed MAC address. Finally, bring the interface back up with the up option for the change to take place.

IP Addresses assignment

Linux has a Dynamic Host Configuration Protocol (DHCP) server that runs a daemon, a process that runs in the background, called dhcpd, or the dhcp daemon. The DHCP server will carry out the assignment of IP addresses to all of the systems that are located on the subnet. It also keeps a log of which IP address is allocated to which machine at any one time. This makes it an excellent resource for forensic analysts to trace hackers after an attack. For that reason, it's useful to understand how the DHCP server works. Usually, to connect to the internet from a LAN, you must have a DHCP-assigned IP.

Therefore, after setting a static IP address, you must return and get a new DHCP-assigned IP address. To do this, you can always reboot your system, but I will show you how to retrieve a new DHCP without having to shut your system down and restart it. To request an IP address from DHCP, all that is required is to call the DHCP server using dhclient followed by an interface that you wish to assign the address. The different Linux distros use different DHCP clients. Kali, for instance, is based on Debian that uses dhclient.

Manipulating the Domain Name System (DNS)

Hackers can find a treasure trove of information on a target in its Domain Name

System (DNS). DNS is a critical component of the internet, and although it's designed to translate domain names to IP addresses, a hacker can use it to garner information on the target.

- **Examining DNS with dig**

DNS is the service that translates a domain name like google.com to the appropriate IP address. This way, your system knows how to get to it. Without DNS, It would mean that we would be required to remember the thousands of IP addresses that belong to the websites we visit frequently. Dig is one of the commands any aspiring hacker needs to know. It offers a way to gather DNS information about a target domain. The stored DNS information can be a crucial piece of early reconnaissance to obtain before attacking. This information could include the IP address of the target's nameserver (the server that translates the target's name to an IP address), the target's email server, and potentially any subdomains and IP addresses. You can also use the dig command to get information on email servers connected to a domain by adding the mx option (mx is short for mail exchange server). This information is critical for attacks on email systems.

- **Changing Your DNS Server**

In some cases, you may want to use another DNS server. To do so, you will edit a plaintext file named /etc/resolv.conf on the system. Open that file in a text editor. Then, on your command line, enter the precise name of your editor followed by the location of the file and the filename.

Wi-Fi Networks

Firstly, let us look at WiFi. Before doing so, here is a small introduction to the various WiFi security protocols that usually are frequently used. The original, Wired Equivalent Privacy (WEP), was severely flawed and easily cracked. Its replacement, WiFi Protected Access (WPA), was a bit more secure. Finally, WPA2PSK, which is much more secure and uses a preshared key (PSK) that all users share, is now used by nearly all WiFi AP's (except enterprise WiFi).

Basic Wireless Commands

ifconfig

To perform a network interface configuration in Unix-based operating systems, one needs ifconfig. It is an administration utility that is found in the system. Ifconfig has utilities that are utilized in the configuration, querying, and controlling of the parameters of the TCP/IP interface. As an interactive tool, ifconfig can be used to show settings of the network interface and analyze them.

In summary, ifconfig does the following:

- The command enables the viewing of settings of a network.
- Carrying out enabling of a network Interface and also disabling it
- Network Interface IP address assigning
- Assigning network interfaces a netmask
- Allocating a Broadcast to Network Interface
- Assigning an IP, Netmask, and Broadcast to Network Interface
- Changing MTU for a Network Interface
- Enabling and disabling Promiscuous Mode
- Addition and removal of New Alias to Network Interface
- Changing the MAC address of Network Interface

iwlist

This command can be used for scanning wireless networks available and also for displaying any other information about the wireless networks which are not displayed when the iwconfig command is used. Iwlist is utilized in the generation of wireless access points that are nearby together with their SSIDs and their MAC addresses.

iwspy

This command is used for monitoring nodes in a network. It can also be used for recording the link quality of the nodes.

ifrename

This command is used for renaming wireless network interfaces depending on multiple criteria that are static to allocate names consistently to each interface. The interface names usually are dynamic by default. This command helps users decide the name of the network interface. The command needs to be executed before bringing the interfaces up.

iwgetid

This is used in the reporting of the NWID, ESSID, or address of the access point of the wireless network presently being used. By default, iwgetid will display the devices' ESSID. Suppose that it is unavailable, it will output its NWID instead. The information reported is the same as the one shown by iwconfig. In comparison, it is easier to do integration in various scripts.

Detecting and Connecting to Bluetooth

In recent times, nearly all gadgets, systems, and devices have inbuilt Bluetooth. The devices can be computers, iPods, smartphones, speakers, game controllers, keyboards, tablets, among others. The ability to break into Bluetooth networks can result in the compromising of the information on the device, assuming a devices' control, and acquisition of a platform to transmit privileges information from and to the device, among other things. We, therefore, need to understand how Bluetooth works if we are to exploit this technology. From this book, you will be able to acquire some basic knowledge that will come in handy during the scanning and connecting to Bluetooth devices in preparation for hacking them.

How Bluetooth Works

First, we can define Bluetooth as a wireless communication technology that enables devices to transmit voice or data wirelessly. This happens over a relatively short distance. This technology was meant to replace the ubiquitous cables that were being used to connect devices while still securing the communications across them. The process of joining two Bluetooth devices is known as pairing. Pretty much any two devices can pair if they are set to a discoverable mode. In the discoverable mode, a Bluetooth device will broadcast the following information about themselves:

- Technical information
- Name
- List of services
- Class

Upon pairing, two Bluetooth devices will exchange a link key. The devices will store the key to be used in the identification of the other device in future pairings. Every device has a unique identifier and usually a manufacturer-assigned name. These will be useful pieces of data when we want to identify and access a device.

Bluetooth Scanning and Reconnaissance

Linux has an implementation of the Bluetooth protocol stack called BlueZ that we are going to use to scan for Bluetooth signals. Most Linux distributions, including Kali Linux, have it as an inbuilt feature by default. BlueZ possesses utilities that can help us scan and manage Bluetooth capable devices. Examples of the utilities are outlined below:

- hciconfig; this is an equivalent of ifconfig in Linux, but made for Bluetooth capable devices.
- hcitool; this is a tool that we use to perform inquiries. The inquiries can be the device ID, name, class, or even

105

its clock information. This helps the devices to work in sync.

- hcidump; sniffing of Bluetooth communications is carried out by this tool, it, therefore, gives us a chance to capture data that is being sent over the Bluetooth signal.

The first scanning and reconnaissance step with Bluetooth is to check whether the Bluetooth adapter on the system that we are using is recognized and enabled so we can use it to scan for other devices.

Scanning for Bluetooth Devices with hcitool

Now that we know our adapter is up, we can use another tool in the BlueZ suite called hcitool, which is used to scan for other Bluetooth devices within range.

With the simple scan command, we can find out Bluetooth devices that are transmitting using their discover beacons. That is, the devices set to their discovery mode. Most of the tools for Bluetooth hacking you are likely to encounter will be using these commands in a script. You should be able to create your tools from these commands using Python script or even bash script.

Using the sdptool to scanning for services

The service discovery protocol, SDP as it is commonly known, is a protocol of Bluetooth that is used in the searching of Bluetooth services (Bluetooth is a suite of services), and, helpfully, BlueZ provides the sdptool tool for browsing a device for the services it offers. It is also important to note that the device does not have to be in discovery mode to be scanned. The syntax is as follows:

sdptool browse MACaddress

Seeing Whether the Devices Are Reachable with l2ping

Once we have gathered the MAC addresses of all nearby devices, we can send out pings to these devices, whether they are in discovery mode or not, to see whether they are in reach. This lets us know whether they are active and within range. To send out a ping, we use the l2ping command with the following syntax:

l2ping MACaddress

Summary

Wireless devices represent the future of connectivity and hacking. Linux has developed specialized commands for scanning and connecting to Wi-Fi APs in the first step toward hacking those systems. The aircrack-ng suite of wireless hacking tools includes both airmon-ng and airodump-ng, which enable us to scan and gather vital information from in-range wireless devices. The BlueZ suite includes hciconfig, hcitool, and other tools capable of scanning and information gathering, which are necessary for hacking the Bluetooth devices within range. It also includes many other tools worth exploring.

Chapter : 7
Cryptography

There are so much mathematics and algorithms in encryption, and that is a topic we would not rather venture into at this point. The explanations will be quite simple and surprisingly easy to understand. We are going to look at the basic concepts and terminologies so that you will be in a position to know some related topics whenever they come up. These include wireless cracking, password cracking, encryption technologies, and hashing. My intention, however, is not to make a cryptographer out of you here. It is a skill that requires time to hone, but to help familiarize the beginner with the terms and concepts of cryptography to help you become a credible hacker.

A Word About Key Size

Key size matters a lot when it comes to cryptography. More secure encryptions have larger keys. A 256-bit key AES is therefore much stronger as compared to a 128-bit key AES. That means it is also much difficult to break it. It suffices to say that in encryption that employs the use of a similar algorithm, the larger the size of the key, the stronger the encryption will be. However, note that the encryptions' strength is based on the key size and the specifics of the algorithm as well. This, therefore, does not imply that larger keys denote stronger encryption between the various encryption algorithms. Let's get started by breaking encryption into categories.

Types of Cryptography

Below are the kinds of encryptions we are going to concentrate on in this book.

- Asymmetric Encryption
- Symmetric Encryption

In this book, however, we are going to focus on symmetric and asymmetric encryption.

Symmetric Cryptography

Here, both the sender and receiver possess similar keys. Symmetric cryptography is undoubtedly the commonly used form of cryptography today. Picture this; you encrypt a message using a password. Supposing I have the same password, I will be able to access the encrypted message. Any other person will not read that message. See how easy that is! This type of cryptography is high-speed and is well suited for streaming applications or bulk storage. A major stumbling block with this method of cryptography is the key exchange. As in the example we have seen above, if we have two ends requiring similar keys, what they need is another third channel that can be used to exchange the keys. This is where symmetric cryptography has its biggest weakness. Assume the entities intending to exchange messages are miles apart, how then, can the key be exchanged. As you may already be aware, the aspect of confidentiality arises. The entities can decide to exchange the key via email, mail, telephone, and so on. That makes it possible to intercept the key that is being exchanged, and as such, the encryptions' confidentiality will be compromised. We have many symmetric algorithms currently in use. The common ones are briefly discussed below.

1 DES – Developed by IBM, DES was among the pioneer encryption schemes. Later own, DES was discovered to possess flaws and was breakable as well. It was DES encryption that was used in hashing early systems of LANMAN originally (pre-2000).

2 3DES – It is the flaws in DES that occasioned the development of this encryption algorithm. It works by a triple application of the DES hence its name. That makes it a bit more secure when compared to DES.

3 AES – In full, AES stands for Advanced Encryption Standard. Cryptographically speaking, AES is not an encryption algorithm by itself. It was NIST that developed AES. It is one of the most robust encryption in use today. AES utilizes the 128-, 196-, and 256-bit keys. Since 2001, AES has been occupied by the Rijndael algorithm. This standard is commonly used in SSL/TLS, WPA2 among other protocols that need speed and confidentiality.

4 RC4 - This does encryption of each bit or byte instead of a single block of information. This is called streaming. RC4 was designed and created by RSAs' Rivest Ronald. This method of encryption is commonly used in WEP and VoIP applications.

5 Blowfish – Blowfish utilizes a key with a varying length. It is a very secure encryption scheme. It is

additionally open-source and as such anyone can be able to use it without a license.

6 Twofish – It is similar to Blowfish. It, however, possesses advanced capabilities such as the use of the 128 or 256-bit key. Twofish was at some point, a strong contender for AES. Examples of applications using Twofish include cryptcat and OpenPGP, among others. Additionally, it is not patented, just like Twofish.

Asymmetric Cryptography

This type of cryptography utilizes different keys for the two ends of the channel of communication. It is an astonishingly slow technique that when compared to symmetric cryptography, is about a thousand times slower! It is, therefore, an undesirable method for use where bulk encryption or streaming communication is concerned. On a positive note, it solves the problem of key exchange. This is because there is no need for having the same keys at both ends of a communication. This type of cryptography is predominantly utilized in cases where two entities need to exchange information but are unknown to each other. The information being transferred here usually is in the form of small bits, for instance, identifying information, i.e., a certificate or a key. Due to limitations in speed, asymmetric cryptography is not generally used for bulk or streaming-encryption. Below are some schemes found under asymmetric encryption.

1 Diffie-Hellman – Without any doubt, Diffie-Hellman key exchange can be said to be the most exceptional development in cryptography. Diffie and Hellman came up with a method of key generation. This effectively eradicated the problem of key exchange that is often a characteristic of symmetric key encryption.

2 RSA – This is an abbreviation for Rivest, Shamir, and Adleman. This scheme makes use of a method where very large prime numbers are factorized. The result is used as the relationship between the two keys.

3 PKI – this is a Public key infrastructure mainly used for exchanging confidential information in an asymmetric system. PKI makes use of a public key alongside a private key.

4 ECC – this is short for Elliptical curve cryptography. The scheme is slowly but surely gaining popularity in the world of mobile computing. This is because it is efficient and also requires minimal energy consumption and computing power to provide a similar level of security. The scheme is dependent on the relationship that is shared by two functions that are located on the same elliptical curve.

5   PGP – an abbreviation for Pretty Good Privacy that
    makes use of encryption that asymmetric for purposes
    of ensuring the integrity and privacy of email
    messages.

Data Security

For us to minimize unauthorized access to databases,
websites, and computers, we need measures that can
safeguard digital privacy. These measures are what we call
data security. It serves to guard data against corruption. For
all organizations, big and small alike, data security is a crucial
IT aspect. Sometimes it can be referred by the name computer
security or information security. Common technologies used
for data security comprise data masking, backups, and also
data erasure among many others. Encryption is also a data
security technology that is essential in safeguarding the
privacy of data as we have said. Here, hardware, software,
hard drives, and digital data are encrypted. This is to make
sure that they are unreadable to hackers and other users. Here
we are talking about those who are unauthorized that may get
their hands on the hardware or software.

Authentication is one way of practicing data security. It is
likely that you have encountered a scenario where you needed
a password to log into your device or even to access your
email. Users must provide identifying credentials such as

biometric data, a password, a username, and so on to do a verification of their identities before granting them access to data or a system.

Digital Certificates

A digital certificate is used in the authentication of the web credentials of a particular sender. The certificate also allows the receiving entity of an encrypted message to get to understand that the data is from a source that is trusted. A certification authority issues the digital certificate. Message encryption and self-signatures use digital certificates. Identity certificates or public key certificates is the other name we use for digital certificates. X.509 is an example of a commonly used digital certificate.

Chapter : 8
Cyber Security

The crondaemon and the crontable (crontab) are the most useful tools for scheduling regular tasks. The first, crond, is a daemon that runs in the background. The crondaemon checks the crontable for which commands to run at specified times. We can alter the crontable to schedule a task or job to execute regularly on a particular day or date, at a particular time daily, or every so many week or months.

To schedule these tasks or jobs, enter them into the crontable file, located at /etc/crontab. The crontable has seven fields: the first five are used to schedule the time to run the task, the sixth field specifies the user, and the seventh field is used for the absolute path to the command you want to execute. If we were using the crontable to schedule a script, we could simply put the absolute path to the script in the seventh field.

Each of the five time fields represents a different element of time: the minute, hour, day of the month, month, and day of the week, in that order. Every element of time must be represented numerically, so March is represented as 3 (you cannot simply input "March"). Days of the week begin at 0, which is Sunday, and end at 7, which is also Sunday. Table 16•1 summarizes this

Table 16•1: Time Representations for Use in the crontab

Field	Time unit	Representation
1	Minute	0–59
2	Hour	0–23
3	Day of the month	1–31
4	Month	1–12

So, if we had written a script to scan the globe for vulnerable open ports and wanted it to run every night at 2:30 AM, Monday through Friday, we could schedule it in the crontab file. We will walk through the process of how to get this information into the crontab shortly, but first let's discuss the format we need to follow, shown in Listing 16• 1.

M H DOM MON DOW USER COMMAND 30 2 * * 1•5 root /root/myscanningscript

Listing 16•1: The format for scheduling commands

The crontab file helpfully labels the columns for you. Note that the first field provides the minute (30), the second field provides the hour (2), the fifth field provides the days (1-5, or Monday through Friday), the sixth field defines the user (root), and the seventh field is the path to the script. The third and fourth fields contain asterisks (*) because we want this script to run every day Monday through Friday regardless of the day of the month or the month.

In Listing 16•1, the fifth field defines a range for the day of the week by using a dash (-) between the numbers. If you want to execute a script on multiple noncontiguous days of the week, you can separate those days with commas (,). Thus, Tuesday and Thursday.

To edit crontab, you can run the crontabcommand followed by the -e(edit) option:

kali >crontab-e

Select an editor. To change later, run 'select•editor'.

/bin/nano <•••• easiest

/usr/bin/mcedit

/usr/bin/vim.basic

/usr/bin/vim.gtk

/usr/bin/vim.tiny Choose 1•5 [1]:

The first time you run this command, it will ask which editor you would like to use. The default is /bin/nano, the 1 option. If you choose this option, it will open directly to

crontab.

Another option, and often a better one for the newcomer to Linux, is to open crontab directly in your favorite text editor, which you can do like so:

kali >leafpad/etc/crontab

I've used this command to open crontab in Leafpad. You can see a snippet of the file in Listing 16•2.

/etc/crontab: system•wide crontab

Unlike any other crontab, you don't have to run the 'crontab' command to install the new version when you edit this file and files in /etc/cron.d. These files also have username fields, which no other crontabs do.

SHELL=/bin/sh

PATH=/usr/local/sbin:/usr/local/bin:/sbin:/bin:/usr/sbi
n:/usr/bin

m h dom mon dow user command

17 * * * * root cd / && run•parts • •report /etc/cron.hourly

25 6 * * * root test •x /usr/sbin/anacron II (cd / && run•parts

47 6 * * 7 root test •x /usr/sbin/anacron II (cd / && run•parts

52 6 1 * * root test •x /usr/sbin/anacron II (cd / && run•parts

#

Listing 16•2: The crontab file in use in a text editor

Now, to set a new regularly scheduled task, you simply need
to enter a new line and save the file.

Scheduling a Backup Task

Let's view this utility first from the system administrator's
perspective. As a system administrator, you'd often want to
run backups of all your files after hours, while the system is
not being used and resources are readily available. (System
backups tend to require system resources that are in short
demand during business hours.) The ideal time might be in

the middle of the night on the weekend. Rather than having to log in at 2 AM on Saturday night/Sunday morning (I'm sure you have other priorities at that

time), you could schedule the backup to start automatically at that time, even though you're not at your computer.

Note that the hour field uses a 24•hour clock rather than using AM and PM, so 1 PM is, for example, 13:00. Also, note that the days of the week (DOW) start with Sunday (0) and end with Saturday (6).

To create a job, you simply need to edit the crontab file by adding a line in the prescribed format. So, say you wanted to create a regular backup job using a user account named "backup." You would write a script for backing up the system and save it as systembackup.sh in the /bin directory, then schedule this backup to run every Saturday night/Sunday morning at 2 AM by adding the following line to crontab:

00 2 * * 0 backup /bin/systembackup.sh

Note that the *wildcard is used to indicate "any," and using it in place of a digit for the day of the month, month, or day of the week is read as "all" days or months. If you read across this line, it says

At the top of the hour (00),

Of the second hour (2),

Of any day of the month (*),

Of any month (*),

On Sunday (0),

As the backup user,

Execute the script at /bin/systembackup.sh.

The crondaemon will then execute that script every Sunday morning at 2 AM, every month.

If you only wanted the backup to run on the 15th and 30th of every month, regardless of what days of the week those dates fell on, you could revise the entry in crontab to appear as follows:

00 2 15,30 * * backup /root/systembackup.sh

Note that the day of the month (DOM) field now has 15,30. This tells the system to run the script only on the 15th and 30th of every month, so around every two weeks. When you want to specify multiple days, hours, or months, you need to list them separated by a comma, as we did here.

Next, let's assume the company requires you to be especially vigilant with its backups.

It can't afford to lose even a day of data in the event of a power outage or system crash.

You would then need to back up the data every weeknight by adding the following line:

00 23 * * 1•5 backup /root/systembackup.sh

This job would run at 11 PM (hour 23), every day of the month, every month, but only on Monday through Friday (days 1–5). Especially note that we designated the days Monday through Friday by providing an interval of days (1-5) separated by a dash (-). This could have also been designated as 1,2,3,4,5;, either way, works perfectly fine.

Using crontab to Schedule Your MySQLscanner

Now that you understand the basics of scheduling a job with the crontabcommand, let's schedule the MySQLscanner.sh script, which seeks out open MySQL ports, that you built in Chapter 8. This scanner searches for systems running MySQL by looking for open port 3306.

To enter your MySQLscanner.sh to the crontab file, edit the file to provide the particulars of this job, just as we did with the system backups. We'll schedule it to run during the day while you're at work so it doesn't take up resources when you're using your home system. To do this, enter the following line in your crontab:

00 9 * * * user /usr/share/MySQLsscanner.sh

We've set up the job to run at 00 minutes, at the ninth hour, every day of the month (*), every month (*), every day of the week (*), and to run it as a regular user. We simply need to save this crontab file to schedule the job.

Now, let's say you wanted to be particularly careful and only run this scanner on weekends and at 2 AM when it's less likely that anyone is watching the network traffic. You also only want it to run in the summer, June through August. Your job would now look like this:

00 2 * 6•8 0,6 user /usr/share/MySQLsscanner.sh

You would add this to your crontab like so:

/etc/crontab: system•wide crontab

Unlike any other crontab, you don't have to run the 'crontab' command to install the new version when you edit this file and files in /etc/cron.d. These files also have username fields, which none of the other crontabs do.

SHELL=/bin/sh

PATH=/usr/local/sbin:/usr/local/bin:/sbin:/bin:/usr/sbin:/usr/bin

m h dom mon dow user command

17 * * * * root cd / && run•parts • •report /etc/cron.hourly

25 6 * * * root test •x /usr/sbin/anacron II (cd / && run•parts • •report /etc/cron.daily)

47 6 * * 7 root test •x /usr/sbin/anacron II (cd / && run•parts • •report /etc/cron.weekly)

52 6 1 * * root test •x /usr/sbin/anacron II (cd / && run•parts • •report /etc/cron.monthly)

002*6-80,6user/usr/share/MySQLsscanner.sh

Now, your MySQLscanner.sh will only run on weekends in June, July, and August at 2 AM.

crontab Shortcuts

The crontab file has some built•in shortcuts you can use instead of specifying the time, day, and month every time. These include the following:

@yearly

@annually

@monthly

@weekly

@daily

@midnight

@noon

@reboot

So, if you wanted the MySQL scanner to run every night at midnight, you could add the following line to the crontab file:

@midnight   user /usr/share/MySQLsscanner.sh

Using Rc Scripts to Run Jobs at Startup

Whenever you start your Linux system, a number of scripts are run to set up the environment for you. These are known as the rc scripts. After the kernel has initialized and loaded all its modules, the kernel starts a daemon known as initor init.d. This daemon then begins to run a number of scripts found in /etc/init.d/rc. These scripts include commands for starting many of the services necessary to run your Linux system as you expect.

Linux Runlevels

Linux has multiple runlevels that indicate what services should be started at bootup. For instance, runlevel 1 is single•user mode, and services such as networking are not started in runlevel 1. The rc scripts are set to run depending on what runlevel is selected:

0 Halt the system

1 Single•user/minimal mode

2–5 Multiuser modes

6 Reboot the system

Adding Services to rc.d

You can add services for the rc.d script to run at startup using the update-rc.dcommand. This command enables you to add or remove services from the rc.d script. The syntax

for update-rc.dis straightforward; you simply list the command followed by the name of the script and then the action to perform, like so:

kali>update-rc.d<nameofthescriptorservice>
<remove | defaults | disable | enable>

As an example of how you can use update-rc.d, let's assume you always want the PostgreSQL database to start upon system boot so that your Metasploit framework can use it to store pentesting and hacking results. You would use update-rc.d to add a line to your rc.d script to have it up and running every time you boot your system.

Before you do that, let's check whether PostgreSQL is running on your system already. You can do so using the pscommand and piping it to a filter looking for PostgreSQL using grep, like so:

kali >psaux | greppostgresql

root 3876   0.0   0.0 12720   964pts/1   S+ 14.24 0.00
grep postgresql

This output tells us that the only process psfound running for PostgreSQL was the very command we ran looking for it, so there is no PostgreSQL database running on this system presently.

Now, let's update our rc.d to have PostgreSQL run automatically at bootup:

kali >update-rc.dpostgresqldefaults

This adds the line to the rc.d file. You need to reboot the system for the change to take place. Once you've done that, let's again use the pscommand with grepto look for a PostgreSQL process:

kali >psaux | greppostgresql

postgresql 757 0.0 0.1 287636 25180 ? S March 14 0.00 /usr/lib/postgresql/9.6/bin/postgresql   •D /var/lib/postgresql/9.6/main

•c config_file=/etc/postgresql/9.6/main/postgresql.conf

root 3876   0.0   0.0 12720   964pts/1   S+ 14.24 0.00 grep postgresql

As you can see, PostgreSQL is running without you ever entering any commands

manually. It automatically starts when your system boots up, ready and waiting to be used with your Metasploit!

Adding Services to Your Bootup via a GUI

If you're more comfortable working from a GUI to add services at startup, you can download the rudimentary GUI•based tool rcconf from the Kali repository, like so:

kali >apt-getinstallrcconf

Once it has completed its installation, you can start rcconf by entering the following:

kali >rcconf

This will open a simple GUI like the one in Figure 16•1. You can then scroll through the

available services, select the ones you want to start upon bootup and click OK.

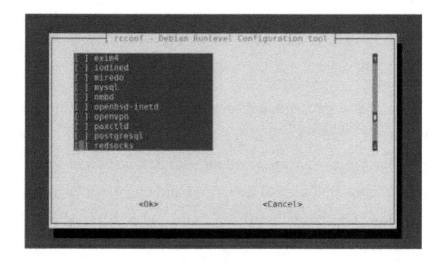

Figure 16•1: The rcconf GUI for adding services to startup

In this figure, you can see the PostgreSQL service listed second from last. Press the spacebar to select this service, press TAB to highlight <Ok>, and then press ENTER. The next time you boot Kali, PostgreSQL will start automatically.

Summary

Both system administrators and hackers often need to schedule services, scripts, and

utilities to run at regular intervals. Linux enables you to schedule nearly any script or utility to run on a regular basis using the crondaemon, which runs these jobs from the crontable. In addition, you can have services start automatically at bootup by using the command update-rc.dor the GUI•based tool rcconf to update the rc.d scripts.

Using pip

Python has a package manager specifically for installing and managing Python packages known as pip (Pip Installs Packages). Since we are working with Python 3 here, you will need pip for Python 3 to download and install packages. You can download and install pip from the Kali repository by entering the following:

 kali >apt-getinstallpython3-pip

Now, to download modules from PyPI, you can simply enter this:

kali >pip3install<packagename>

When you download these packages, they are automatically placed in the /usr/local//lib/<python•version>/dist•packages directory. So, for instance, if you had used pip to install the Python implementation of the SNMP protocol for Python 3.6, you would find it at /usr/local/lib/python3.6/pysnmp. If you aren't sure where a package has been placed on your system (sometimes, different distributions of Linux use different directories), you can enter pip3 followed by show and the package name, as shown here:

kali >pip3showpysnmp

Name: pysnmp

Version: 4.4.4

Summary: SNMP library for Python

Home•page: https://github.com/etingof/pysnmp

Author: Ilya Etingof <etingof@gmail.com>

Author•email: etingof@gmail.com

License: BSD

Location: usr/local/lib/python3.6/dist•packages

Requires: ptsmi, pyansl, pycryptodomex

You can see this gives you a lot of information about the package, including the directory that holds it.

As an alternative to using pip, you can download a package directly from the site (make certain that is downloaded to the proper directory), unpack it (see Chapter 9 on how to unpack software), and then run the following:

kali >pythonsetup.pyinstall

This will install any unpacked packages that haven't yet been installed.

Installing Third-Party Modules

To install a third•party module created by another member of the Python community (as opposed to an officially released Python package), you can simply use wget to download it from wherever it is being stored online, uncompress the module, and then

run the pythonsetup.pyinstallcommand.

As an example, let's download and install the Python module for the port•scanning tool we used in Chapter 8, nmap, from its online repository at https://xael.org.

First, we need to download the module from xael.org:

kali   >wgethttp://xael.org/norman/python/python-nmap/python-nmap-0.3.4.tar.gz ••2014•12•28 17:48:32•• http://xael.org/norman/python/python•nmap/python•nmap• 0.3.4.tar.gz

Resolving xael.org (xael.org)...194.36.166.10

Connecting to xael.org (xael.org)|194.36.166.10|:80...connected.

••snip••

2018•21•28 17.48:34 (113 KB/s) • 'python•nmap•0.3.4.tar.gz' saved [40307/40307]

Here, you can see we use the wgetcommand and the full URL for the package. After the package has downloaded, you need to uncompress it with tar, as you learned:

kali >tar-xzfpython-nmap-0.3.4.tar.gz

Then change directories to the newly created directory:

kali >cdpython-nmap-.03.4/

Finally, in that directory, install the new module by entering the following:

kali >~/python-nmap-0.3.4>pythonsetup.pyinstall

running install

running build

running build_py

creating build

••snip••

running install_egg_info

writing
/usr/local/lib/python2.7/dist•packages/python_nmap•0.3.
4.egg.info

Innumerable other modules can be obtained this way as well. Once you've installed this nmap module, you can use it in your Python scripts by importing the module. More on this later. Now let's get started on some scripting.

Chapter : 9
Virtual Private Network and Firewall

Virtual Private Networks

Using a virtual private network can be an effective way to keep your web traffic relatively anonymous and secure. A VPN is used to connect to an intermediary internet device such as a router that sends your traffic to its ultimate destination tagged with the IP address of the router. Using a VPN can certainly enhance your security and privacy, but it is not a guarantee of anonymity. The internet device you connect to must record or log your IP address to be able to send the data back to you accurately, so anyone able to access these records can uncover information about you.

The beauty of VPNs is that they are simple and easy to work with. You can open an account with a VPN provider and then seamlessly connect to the VPN each time you log on to your computer. You would use your browser as usual to navigate the web, but it will appear to anyone watching that your traffic is coming from the IP address and location of the internet VPN device and not your own. Besides, all traffic between you and the VPN device is encrypted, so even your internet service provider cannot see your traffic.

Among other things, a VPN can be useful in evading government-controlled Content and information censors. For instance, if your national government limits your access to websites with particular political messages, you can likely use a VPN based outside your country to access that Content. Some media corporations, such as Netflix, limit access to their Content to IP addresses originating from their nation. Using a VPN based in a country that those services allow can often get you around those access limitations. Some of the best VPN services are: IPVanish, NordVPN, ExpressVPN, CyberGhost, Golden Frog VPN, Hide My Ass, Private Internet Access, PureVPN, TorGuard, and Buffered VPN

The strength of a VPN is that all your traffic is encrypted when it leaves your computer, thus protecting you against snooping, and your IP address is cloaked by the VPN IP address when you visit a site. As with a proxy server, the owner of the VPN has your originating IP address.

Using a virtual private network can be an effective way to keep your web traffic relatively anonymous and secure. A VPN is used to connect to an intermediary internet device such as a router that sends your traffic to its ultimate destination tagged with the IP address of the router. Using a VPN can certainly enhance your security and privacy, but it's not a guarantee of anonymity. The internet device you connect to must record or log your IP address to be able to send the data back to you accurately, so anyone able to access these records can uncover information about you.

The beauty of VPNs is that they are simple and easy to work with. You can open an account with a VPN provider and then seamlessly connect to the VPN each time you log on to your computer. You would use your browser as usual to navigate the web, but it will appear to anyone watching that your traffic is coming from the IP address and location of the internet VPN device and not your own. Besides, all traffic between you and the VPN device is encrypted, so even your internet service provider can't see your traffic.

Among other things, a VPN can be useful in evading government-controlled Content and information censors. For instance, if your national government limits your access to websites with a particular political message, you can likely use a VPN based outside your country to access that Content. Some media corporations, such as Netflix, limit access to their Content to IP addresses originating from their nation. Using a VPN based in a country that those services allow can often get you around those access limitations. Some of the best VPN services are: IPVanish, NordVPN, ExpressVPN, CyberGhost, Golden Frog VPN, Hide My Ass, Private Internet Access, PureVPN, TorGuard, and Buffered VPN

The strength of a VPN is that all your traffic is encrypted when it leaves your computer, thus protecting you against snooping, and your IP address is cloaked by the VPN IP address when you visit a site. As with a proxy server, the owner of the VPN has your originating IP address.

Firewall

A firewall is a protective system that secures a network by filtering incoming and outgoing traffic. The firewall's user defines a set of rules, which the firewall follows. These rules define what traffic is allowed in and out of the system. Firewalls block every data packet that isn't explicitly allowed in their configuration.

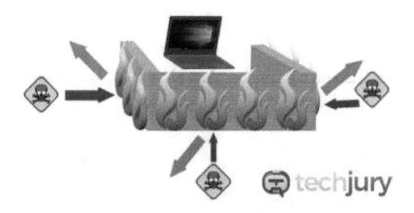

The firewall isn't a silver bullet but combined with other security solutions, it can make a system nearly invincible to attacks. If you want better network security, a firewall is a must – **it can block most attacks** originating outside of the network.

Now that you know what a firewall is, we can delve deeper to see how it actually works.

What Does a Firewall Do?

In essence, a firewall's work is relatively simple. The user defines what traffic is okay to pass through and what isn't. Generally, it enforces three simple commands – drop, reject, or accept/allow access to the network.

Here's what they do:

- Drop – The data packet trying to enter or leave the system is blocked directly.

141

- Reject – The same as the drop command, but the sender of the data will receive an error message.
- Accept/Allow – The data packet will be able to go through the firewall.

These three commands operate thanks to predefined rules. When users establish a new firewall, they configure what traffic could reach the network or leave it.

The firewall can block (or allow) access based not only on **IP addresses, but also domain names, keywords, protocols, ports,** and **apps.**

For example, you can configure a firewall's settings to accept traffic from an employee's home IP address only. That way, if the same employee tried to connect to your network from a café, he would be blocked.

The firewall checks every data packet according to the predefined rules. If you've added 10 trusted IP addresses, the firewall will **block all packets,** coming from IPs **outside the list.** In case there are several rules, each connection will have to pass successfully through **every one** of them.

Generally, a user can't predict every possible connection. So for a firewall to work whenever the specific rules don't apply, there's a **default policy** in place.

Firewall Default Policy

If your firewall security solution receives a data packet for which user-generated rules don't apply, the default policy comes into play. In such a case, it performs only one of the three commands mentioned above.

Let's assume the firewall default policy is set to "**allow.**" That means every connection, besides the explicitly forbidden ones, is approved. This is actually a lousy security protocol since in this case, malicious data packets can easily infiltrate the network.

If the default policy is set to **"drop,"** it will neglect all connections that don't match the rules.

Now.

There's a difference in how a firewall reacts to traffic. There's **incoming** and **outgoing** traffic, thus different rules for both.

Typically, outgoing traffic is always allowed, since it comes from a presumably trusted source – your server.

However, there should be some limitations, since a cybercriminal can, in theory, overtake the server. If you think that could be the case, you wouldn't want untrusted communication (like sharing sensitive data) going out.

The network firewall treats incoming traffic in a different way – there's a need for a whole bunch of rules for each specific case. Maximizing the security benefits of a firewall could be a tiresome job.

This is a simplified example of configuring firewall settings:

Since you already have a fairly decent knowledge of what a firewall is, let's see the differences between firewalls of various types.

Types of Firewalls

There isn't like one firewall to rule them all. Firewalls come in different casings and have different ways of filtering the traffic.

There are three most common types of firewalls – **packet filtering, stateful,** and **application-level.**

Packet Filtering

Packet filtering is the first generation of firewalls.

When a firewall uses this method, it checks each data packet on its way into or out of the network. This firewall offers protection by accepting or dropping packets based on the rules defined by the user.

Packet filtering is a decent security option, but definitely not the best. Moreover, it requires a lot of **time and effort** to configure.

Stateful Firewall

Stateful firewalls, also known as **second generation firewalls,** can compare data packets to previous ones. This makes this type of firewall more flexible than the packet filtering ones (also known as **stateless**). Stateful firewalls, in essence, trade speed for better security.

In simple words, stateful firewalls can "remember" data transfers to or from a trusted network, thus applying the firewall rules to the **whole communication.** Packet-filtering, on the other hand, has to measure each data packet against its rules.

Application Level Gateway/Proxy Server Firewall

By now you know that the previous two types of firewall control incoming and outgoing traffic. **The third generation firewall** – application layer, goes a step further and analyzes the data, thus allowing or denying access to specific **applications** (hence its name). It has the ability to block apps and services which don't meet its user-defined policy.

Alright, so those were the three major types of firewalls.

However, this doesn't mean a firewall uses only one of these techniques. In fact, a good network firewall **combines** two or all of these methods to provide a higher level of security.

These approaches are at the core of every software firewall. On top of that, there could be a hardware firewall as well, to improve the firewall security.

Hardware Firewall

The hardware firewalls are usually devices with built-in packet filtering technology. They can be either a **standalone device,** or be implemented in a **broadband router**. Since they are the first line of defense against malicious data, hardware firewalls aim to protect all the systems on a local network by covering its **entry and exit points.**

One of the benefits of hardware firewalls is that they are easy to configure. Once configured, you can test it with any of these free tools: NMAP, Tenable, and Personal Firewall.

Software Firewall

The software firewall, also known as a host-based firewall, is the most common method for protection for individuals. Unlike the hardware firewall, a software firewall protects only the device it's installed on, not the whole network. For better security, it's best to use both, which is called a **network-based firewall.**

Software firewalls allow users to define some of their features but don't offer the full-customization options a hardware firewall does.

Most software firewalls will not only protect you from external threats, but also from some of the most common malicious apps.

As with most security elements, it's vital to keep your firewall up to date.

Next-Generation Firewall

In 2009, the advisory firm Gartner defined the term "next-generation firewall." As the name suggests, it's an improved version of traditional firewalls.

Next-generation firewalls (NGFW) apply their policies for applications, protocols, as well as ports.

Unlike traditional firewalls, the NGFW performs what's called a deep packet inspection (DPI.) This method differs from conventional packet filtering, which checks only the packet header. DPI, on the other hand, examines the data inside a packet to check if the package is safe or not.

Deep packet inspection combines an **intrusion detection system** (IDS), an **intrusion** *prevention* **system** (IPS), and the traditional stateful firewall.

Chapter : 10
Password Cracking

1   Cracking encryptions

Kali Linux was solely designed to be a hacker's or security professional's best tool. We have seen that Kali comes packed with multiple tools and programs not always available on other operating systems. One reason Kali Linux has become so popular is its ability to break wireless encryption standards that are used in securing wireless devices. An example of a wireless device is the router. An attacker can use Kali to break into wireless systems, therefore, gaining themselves full access to the network. The consequences of being hacked may be nominal in a home setting, but more damaging in a

149

professional setting. Let us have a step-by-step look at how you can break WPA and WPA2 by utilizing Kali Linux.

What is needed

Make sure you have the following items together before you begin:

- A computer with Kali Linux installed
- A wireless router configured to use WPA2
- A wireless card that is capable of running in monitor mode
- The aircrack-ng software

The Attack Process

Note that it would be best to have root privileges on the Kali user account you are using to perform the attack. Otherwise, you may have to use the sudo command, which can be extremely tedious.

Step 1

Ensure that your network card is visible in Kali by using the ifconfig command. If you are using a wireless card via USB, make sure that it is plugged in.

Step 2

Ensure that your computer is not currently connected to a wireless network. Then you will need to run the airmon-ng command from the terminal. This command will display all of your wireless interfaces that are capable of running in monitor mode.

Step 3

Now you need to actually start using airmon-ng on your wireless interface. After you have completed this step, the output in the lower-right corner of the terminal should display the listening wireless interface which will likely be named mon0.

Step 4

Next, you will need to run the dump command with the listening wireless interface as a parameter. This will show you any information obtained from wireless networks in range of your wireless cards such as the encryption type, the MAC address of the wireless device (BSSID), and other information such as the channel and model number of the wireless device.

Step 5

Find the wireless network that you want to crack and copy its BSSID. Thereafter, the information obtained from the

151

airodump-ng command will be required to be plugged into the command which is used for starting the procedure of attack. The command we will need to use is as follows:

airodump-ng -c [wireless channel] –bssid [BSSID] -w /root/Desktop/ [monitor interface]

Remember that the monitoring interface as we have said before is likely to be mon0.

Step 6

At this step, your wireless interface will be gathering and storing information about the wireless network, but in order for the attack to succeed, we will need a host to connect to the wireless network. When a device connects to the wireless router, our Kali software will capture data regarding a four-way handshake that is the weak point in the protocol. Alternatively, you can use a de-authorization command. This command will create some de-authorization packets to send to the target wireless router to force the reconnection process for other devices. We will target a device to force to reconnect by using the client's BSSID in command. The only requirement is that you already need to be able to see a connected client's BSSID in the previous command's output.

Step 7

Ensure that you don't close the terminal that you started running the airodump-ng command. Then, start a second terminal and using this command:

aireplay-ng –0 2 –a [Router-BSSID] –c [Client-BSSID] mon0

Step 8

You should now view the output that displays the indication of a successful handshake. If you don't, however, there are a multitude of factors that could have caused it to fail. One common problem is that the wireless signal was too weak, in which case you would only need to move your computer closer towards the wireless router. In addition, the connected device may not be configured to automatically reconnect to the network. If that's the case, then you will have to wait for them to reconnect.

Step 9

Upon a successful reconnection handshake, we are going to need to crack the protocol. Enter the following command, and plug in the parameters as they pertain to your configuration:

aircrack-ng -a2 -b [Router-BSSID] -w [Wordlist-File] /root/Desktop/.cap*

The only new parameter in this command is a wordlist we have not yet discussed. A wordlist is basically a file containing different character combinations that we will use to carry out the attack. You can find them online for free, just make sure you remember where you store the data on your computer and use the file's path as a parameter in the preceding command. After you have entered the command, the software will finally initiate the process of breaking the wireless encryption.

Step 10

All that is needed is to wait for the software to break the key. Note that in order to successfully break the encryption, the Wi-Fi password needs to be contained in the wordlist. This is called a dictionary-based attack, which is a little different from a brute force attack. A dictionary-based attack simply tries all of the passwords in a list or database whereas an attack of brute force fashion will attempt to utilize all the possible character combinations. If your dictionary failed to find the correct password, you can try using an additional wordlist. Also note that it could take a long time to actually break the password, depending on the strength and complexity of the password as well as how fast your computer hardware is.

Step 11

Once the software successfully cracks the password, it will display the key near the middle of the terminal in a line that reads:

KEY FOUND! [wireless key]

Go ahead and try logging in with the key for fun.

Finally...

Breaking WPA and WPA2 encryption are pretty easy as far as security attacks are concerned. But please remember to use this information responsibly as the consequences could be terribly severe.

2 Attacking with Frame Networks

This is the attack type that is also called a de-authentication DoS Attack. Here, the attacker saturates vast amounts of frames in the network that carries out de-authentication. Targets will get disconnected from a wireless network when they receive de-authentication frames. The network users will not be able to maintain a connection if the attack is prolonged. An attacker can launch a de-authentication DoS attack in various ways. Commonly used methods are:

- The attacker can create spoofed de-authentication frames and set the source MAC address as the victim MAC address and destination MAC address as the AP's MAC address. Thus upon receipt of the frame, the AP thinks that a genuine user wishes to leave the network and what follows is disconnection of the particular user.

- The attacker can create spoofed de-authentication frames and set the source MAC address as the AP's MAC address and destination MAC address as victim MAC address and inject these spoofed frames into the network. These spoofed frames upon reaching the user's terminal disconnect the user from the network.

- The attacker can craft a packet with source MAC address of the AP and destination as broadcast MAC address. All the users linked to a particular Access point will get disconnected. A broadcast de-authentication DoS attack has impacts that are so severe to the extent that all users connected to a target access point in the network can be de-authenticated.

An attacker has at his disposal, utilities such as scapy, the aircrack-ng suite, file2air among others that they can use for launching the denial of service de-authentication attack. An attacker just needs a networks' SSID, BSSID of the access point, the targets' MAC address and is good to go. TCPdump, airodump-ng, Wireshark and kismet are some of the tools an attacker can use to obtain this information. A wireless network attacker may opt to insert periods of silence between the transmission of de-authentication frames to evade detection and make the attack more stealthy.

Conclusion

I take this opportunity to thank you for being able to make it to the end of Hacking With Kali Linux. Let's hope it has been edifying and through it, you have been able to accrue the requisite knowledge to enable you to begin your hacking career or improve your skills if you are already one. I sincerely hope that you have enjoyed flipping pages all the way from the first topic which was Basics of Hacking, Cyber Attacks, Linux for Hacking, Basics of Kali, Scanning and Managing Networks, File and Directories Permissions, Cyber Security, Becoming Secure and Anonymous, and finally onto some basics of cryptography. I am also hoping that by studying this book, you have got to learn plenty of practical concepts that you need to become a hacking expert.

By now, you must have been able to get access to a vast body of theoretical knowledge regarding the various types of attacks that can be launched on your systems, the reason for launching them, and how you can safeguard your infrastructure against such attacks. These are your first steps towards becoming a professional hacker. The book covers topical issues like wireless network attacks, cyber-attacks, and penetration testing, among others. It, therefore, means that you are now in an excellent position to discern network attack mechanisms being perpetrated in the real world and recommend appropriate remedial measures.

I have also given you several security measures you can implement to keep your networks safe. The formatting is such that the language is quite user-friendly and that you can understand the importance of securing your systems. Going forward, the next step is to put the concepts you have acquired from this book into practice. They say practice makes perfect, and it is by practicing that one can become a master in the field of hacking, more so using Kali Linux. Let the knowledge you have acquired from the book work for you.

Finally, if you found this book useful in any way, a review on Amazon is always appreciated!